Molly Chronicles:
Serotonin Serenade

by Jim Simons

Plain View Press
P. O. 42255
Austin, TX 78704

plainviewpress.net
sb@plainviewpress.net
1-512-441-2452

Copyright Jim Simons, 2006. All rights reserved.
ISBN: 978-1-891386-75-6
Library of Congress Number: 2006938693

Cover Art by Nancy Simons from a photo by Cris Cunningham.

Author's Foreword

My main motivation for writing this memoir was the belief that the cases I handled were part of the history of the collective efforts of many people which peaked in the '60s but really started before and continued since. In that time we called this wave of activism for social change simply the Movement. I found that writing about the cases required me to write about the people I worked with and the alternative style of our practice–and lives. And that required me to write about my own life in detail and with complete honesty. Also, it is well known that the cultural changes roaring through the '60s included freer sex and usage of drugs. If this material is not interesting or palatable to some readers, they should probably start reading this book around page 43 at the paragraph that starts with "At graduation" (from law school).

I believe that my life and my legal work are integrally entwined and in the Movement days we consciously strived to make it that way. Moreover, a straight recounting of cases would be just another lawyer book. It was the backdrop of an incredibly vibrant time of upheaval, personal and social, and the momentous politics of change–for peace and justice– that make the cases important.

I have to credit Dave Dellinger and his book "From Yale to Jail" as being a model of describing not just the work for change but the life, the living of our convictions, or at least, in my case, trying to live a life dedicated to peace and justice. I never gave a hoot about just being a lawyer–there are a million now in the U.S. (as I learned from Tom Paxton's great song). My story is about the decision I made in late 1967 (or did it go back to public school?) to be a Movement lawyer. Radical politics trumped law easily but I hoped to find a way to serve the former by using the latter. That effort is what this memoir is about.

"So we beat on, boats against the current, borne back ceaselessly into the past."
F. Scott Fitzgerald, ***The Great Gatsby***

With Appreciation

First and foremost always, I thank my wife Nancy who played such a huge role not only in my life and work but in the writing and editing of this book. I can never thank her enough for her support in all we do and for being who she is: her values, honesty and courage. My old and good friend Greg Olds, a writer and editor by profession, was very helpful in so many ways, not least in encouraging me to take the risks involved in baring the soul in print. Texas writers who tried to be helpful (instead of brushing me off) in the frustrating, anguishing search for agents and publishers who would at least read some of the mss.: Jan Reid, Professor Robert Jensen at University of Texas, Dick Reavis and Jim Hightower.

Introduction: The Quadralegal

Not so long ago I faced the big 6-0, my birthday due before the end of the 20th century. It was sobering, though of course at that point I'd been sober for about 20 years. In dog years, Molly was even older than I. She was like 105.

Molly was my sole assistant and staff as I did the last bits of legal work of my 40 years of being a lawyer. When asked if I had a paralegal, I said yes, but she's actually a quadralegal. We were clearing cases, sending letters announcing my retirement, though she noticed that the time frame was a little vague.

Molly is a 13-pound poodle mix: black mostly, long fur that on her underside turns brown in a way that suggests Yorkie blood. She is quite simply the gentlest being I have ever seen.

Sentimental Journey

Molly remains exactly like she was as a puppy: she does the same things, only it takes her a lot longer.

On the other hand, I have become quite different. Different as day and night. It is this phenomenon that occupies me so much. How can a man change so much in only a few decades?

When I was a boy (and possibly a budding depressive), the saddest, scariest thing I could imagine was my mother dying. I had nightmares about it. Somehow I came to associate these morose imaginings with a popular song of the 1940s, "Sentimental Journey." I thought of her being gone, I heard the song in my head and I cried secretly.

My mother's favorite admonition was: Straighten up and fly right. She spoke in a stream of colloquialisms and in an idiom that I'm sure she heard growing up as the youngest of twelve children. For years, I got up in the mornings for school to my mother's morning voice saying: up, up, up, up and at 'em. I relied so much on my mother, who always came through for me, though in my turn I failed her.

Some of my fear of my mother's death arose from a funeral my parents took me to in 1947 when I was eight and my Aunt Ruth died. I saw her dead in the coffin. I was shaken by the experience and it triggered what has been lifelong insomnia.

I can remember brief snatches of life from age 3 or 4. But it seems in the retrospection of late life that it began at age 5 or 6 in Waco during the war. A sense of being alive, of living the days, a hint of the promises and possibilities that I also heard in the rustling of the trees later as a young man in the Texas Hill Country. Magical summer evenings that promised so much more than life delivers along a path from deeply wistful to moodily nostalgic. From six to sixty.

Molly would have liked the dog we had in Waco and Dallas, Stubby: so named because someone had whacked off most of his tail as they sometimes did. (I never learned why.) My dad when he was drunk pretended to tell Stubby jokes in his ear. When the dog panted as dogs do, my dad said he was laughing at the joke. Sometimes he gave Stubby beer in his water bowl.

Even early on in Waco, I was aware that my dad was often drunk, mostly on weekends. My mother took the Baptist view that drinking was wrong, period. She railed against it; he kept on drinking until near the end, a sad New Year's Eve, 1957. He had nearly caught the lifeline of Alcoholics Anonymous weeks before he died but time ran out.

We lived in Waco from 1944 to 1949. I started school there at Provident Heights Elementary; I was in the 5th grade at Sanger Avenue Elementary when we moved to Abilene (for only a few months). All I remember very clearly about the first year in Waco was the death of FDR. It was bigger than winning the war. My parents worshipped the man, as did many, many working-class people all over America. We had a clock that was a 12-inch high bronze statute of FDR at the helm of the Ship of State, the face of the clock inside the round tiller firmly held by our intrepid leader. There was more sadness over the passing of Roosevelt than there was happiness over the war ending that same year, even though the end of the war was the only thing that saved my father from the draft. He was already about 30 but it was said around our house that he would soon be called. Would soon be packing off overseas and we simply accepted that as the reality of the day. But it never happened.

About 1946, I had my own brush with death though it did not scare me. I had pneumonia and was hospitalized. The Baptist hospital was full so I was admitted at Provident Heights, a Catholic hospital. Three times a day a nurse in full habit (the nurses were all nuns) came to give me a penicillin shot in the butt. In those days the needles were big, the penicillin thick and white as sperm. That was the thing I feared, those shots administered by the formidable and fearsome wives of Jesus. My dad gave me a quarter (a week's allowance) every time I did not cry; I got wealthy, for a 7 year old.

It was the first of two times I believe my life has been saved by pharmaceuticals. Then, penicillin was the recently approved wonder drug antibiotic and it saved my life. Three and a half decades later a simple tricyclic antidepressant, generically known as nortriptyline, would save my life, also. When I hear people, often recovered alcoholics, speak disparagingly of prescription drugs, I shudder to think what would have happened to me in 1946 or 1981 without the prescription drugs that allowed me to live.

When I had pneumonia, we lived in one of two houses my parents ever owned. It was in south Waco, not far from Baylor University. It was an eventful year. I discovered there was no Santa Claus by finding his bounty hidden in our garage before Christmas.

The neighborhood we lived in was tough: working class Anglos and Hispanics. There were no gangs, guns or drugs but there was sex and kids my age and older were getting it on. For me it was only a matter of going to a shed somewhere in the neighborhood of small frame homes with mostly older boys where we all masturbated together. Hardly thrilling, it was a matter of breaking the rules, thumbing our noses at Sunday School, tasting the forbidden. Some older guys were actually penetrating the girls in the neighborhood though I had no idea how that worked. I had no clear notion of the sexual apparatus of girls. Boys I had seen: myself and others. My mother and little sister had always been very modest, though seeing them naked, if I had ever been able to, would not have helped much.

In the last couple of years in Waco I had my first girlfriend, Judy Stogdill, who lived right across the alley, her house facing on Morrow Street. On Saturday we went to the 25th Street Theater for a movie and we held hands. Hard to believe now but that was what we did. It was some sort of secret (done only in the darkened theater) signal of affection. I don't think I ever kissed Judy.

I was deeply interested in all matters sexual. I would have this trait throughout life and it would often land me in trouble. There would always be a bit of Protestant guilt, a forbidden mystique associated with sex–and later, with alcohol. Two things I could never leave alone or get enough of. They would in many ways be defining themes for my life. My mother's unswerving allegiance to the Baptist Church and the enforced church attendance never took with me (except for one brief period at age 12).

I was quick to unzip my pants or quaff the mighty elixir whenever I had the chance. It was New Year's Eve of 1946 that I first tasted alcohol at age 7. My parents had a New Year's Eve party for the other union painters (Local No. 53) Daddy worked with. They were a hard-drinking bunch, Shorty Rose and the gang. I surreptitiously tasted people's drinks trying to discover what all the fuss was about this stuff called whiskey and beer. I was disappointed. The few small tastes I got did nothing at all for me.

In fourth grade there was a big but timid kid in my class whose name was Stanley, who was picked on by the other kids. When they started to beat him up on the playground, I interceded, defending Stanley. It was something I did regularly in later life, in courtrooms mostly. If someone was unpopular, I defended him. If she was being picked on by the State, I defended her. If they were poor and powerless with no voice, I stood to speak for them.

I am thankful that I had the innate ability to perceive injustice and to refuse to tolerate it. It came to me from my parents, who strongly identified with underdogs. They were not particularly political, yet they had the right values. My dad was strictly a union painter. From my earliest childhood, I remember nonunion painters being known as "rats." So-in-so was a rat painter. Their love of FDR was genuine in my parents; they were Democrats.

I was in the habit in Waco circa 1948 of getting up in summertime at dawn, mounting my Western Flyer bike and cruising around Gorman and Morrow Streets. I felt great on these fresh, new summer mornings;

I felt I'd gotten the jump on everyone. Life was good. But there was one morning I did not feel good.

The night before my parents had argued loudly and, to my astonishment and anguish, I saw my drunken father hit my mother repeatedly in the face. She cried; my sister and I cried and begged him to stop. It was the ugliest, scariest thing I had ever witnessed in my life. It qualitatively changed how I viewed life. And my dad. A measure of the safety I generally felt left my life forever on that summer evening. The great warmth I felt for my father was qualified: I loved him, sober. Drunk I did not know him. Sober he played catch with me, took me to Waco Pirate baseball and Baylor football games; he taught me to fish in the waters of the Brazos and Bosque Rivers. There was a new and uncomfortable ambivalence in my feelings for my father.

Later, I would regularly stand between him and my mother, protecting her from him. I could not stand by if he became violent. The incident in summer of '48 was the worst it ever was. Usually there was more arguing and cursing, threatening gestures, not much actual physical contact. In standing up to him, protecting my mother (so I thought), I first took the role of hero-child.

At such times my mother regularly said: my consolation is I know Jimmy will never drink; he has seen what it does. And I readily affirmed this prophecy and meant it with all my heart. I told her solemnly as only a child can be solemn: I will never touch a drop of alcohol.

It caused me tremendous anxiety whenever he became abusive to her (but never to my sister and me). I guess my mother was the number one ally in my early strategic alliances. She represented dependable love, safety and direction when the chips were down. Later in my life, long after she was dead, I would believe that she saved my life in a time of deep despair by virtue of the inner strength I inherited from her. I by God meant to keep my promise and never drink booze.

The years we lived in Waco from 1944 to 1949 were a single phase of life for me, and another phase commenced in 1950 in Dallas. I hated to leave Waco, home of the beloved Waco Pirates and Baylor Bears, where there had been more good times than bad on balance.

Skinny

Molly is untroubled by vanity or lust. She is not fat or thin, just right. She was spayed early in the 80's when we got her.

Skinny was the dreaded word used by Linda Sheffield when I was 11 and wanted her in some way, I knew not exactly how. She rejected me as too skinny.

That had been in 1950; all I knew about sex was the manual technique for "feeling good." It might have been an orgasm of sorts but there was not yet sperm, no ejaculation. I had no idea how a pretty girl, like Linda Sheffield, might fit into my craving for sex, but the possibilities were mind-boggling.

In the Dallas of 1950, there was a movie theater way out on Beckley in Oak Cliff where on Saturday I kissed Linda in the dark over and over until the movie ended. A spark ignited and yet I had no real idea of the act of love. My balls ached, there was fire in the loin, but it had no direction.

We had just moved to Dallas, living across the Trinity River in Oak Cliff. I was a fifth grader though school was about to go into summer vacation. My true passion was baseball. I was a Cleveland Indians fan. The tribe had been in the '48 World Series and would be in the '54 series. A good time to be a Cleveland fan, cheering Bob Feller, Larry Doby, Early Wynn, Bob Lemon, Lou Boudreau–many terrific ballplayers. I detested the Yankee juggernaut, and still do. Their teams of the era rolled over everybody, as it seemed then.

I had learned to masturbate at about age 6 and had regularly done it until I became devoutly religious in about 1951, I think partly because of Beverley Scrimshire, who I was attracted to probably only because of proximity. She lived across the street and seemed to be a devout Methodist. I went to her church though my mother had raised me in the Southern Baptist Church, much against my will. The devout religious period left me deeply conflicted over the pleasurable sexual procedure. I knew it was a serious sin but the flesh would not be denied. Moreover, I doubted that Beverley would care for a boy who did such a filthy thing.

My interest in Beverley faded fast without anyone ever knowing about it and was wholly supplanted in summer by the major league season. Soon the devout Christian faith I had acquired in wintertime because of Beverley (and from having heard Billy Graham preach on TV) slipped away, too. I went back to my old self and the procedure, which was, as Woody Allen said, having sex with someone I loved.

We lived right on Zangs Boulevard in Oak Cliff, a street that essentially became Interstate 35. While standing on the front porch rail watching cars streak by, I devised a game called Car Baseball. I got to where I could identify the year and model of every car on the road. Ford and Chevrolet battled it out for supremacy. I also played imaginary baseball games hitting rocks into our neighbor's yard while calling play-by-play. It had to stop when the neighbor objected to the flying rocks.

He had a son a little younger than me. I wanted to be friends with him because they had the only TV on the block. Local programming was terrible but there were some good shows on networks, e.g. Show of Shows with Sid Caesar. We used to see the Howdy Doody Show. The local puppet in Dallas was Webster Webfoot. TV was an exciting new thing after years of the family sitting around a big radio console listening to all the old standards: Fibber McGee and Molly, Jack Benny, My Friend Irma, The FBI, The Shadow, Tom Mix (for me, in afternoons of the '40s), the Lone Ranger. On and on.

I think most of my friends had screwed, or at least screwed around with a steady girlfriend. I had two in high school, girls I went steady with as we said then, for over a year. Allison, a prim little Baptist girl from one of the few affluent pockets in the Adamson high school district, preferred to masturbate me to orgasm in a car or secretly in a back room of her house with her parents unaware. We did copulate on occasion, usually cramped into a car seat, often her little yellow MG convertible. The sex was not notable.

The other girl, Sherry, from the wrong side of the tracks, was a hot-blooded, full-fledged fuck, but only in the missionary position, the only one we knew. Sex with Sherry was stirringly passionate. The kind that turned your toes cherry red (as we used to say) and sent you into orbit for hours after.

We had started dating in 8th grade. There was true chemistry between us from early in our dating, mostly going to movies at the Texas Theater (yes, where Lee Harvey Oswald was apprehended) where we necked endlessly and I became painfully aroused and suffered what we called the "stone aches."

Later, she would skip school, and by design I would come over after her mother left for work. When kissing got to the point of unbearable desire, she allowed me to pull her panties aside at her crotch and enter her. Neither of us knew anything to speak of about contraception. Amazingly, we did not pay the usual price for that, but there were scares, one of which my parents found a note about and became very upset.

At about this time in high school I had managed to get hold of a car key to my parents' 1947 Dodge and I made a duplicate. While my mother was at work at a bank near our house, I would take the Dodge for rides, adventures and flings with Sherry to Kiest Park or for the new delicacy then available at only one place in Oak Cliff, pizza pie. Of course, I got caught and reprimanded but I was unrepentant as always.

Eventually, Sherry and I broke up and she married an older guy with a rap sheet, who threatened me if I ever contacted her and I only did it once.

But soon there was Allison and her sports car in which to ride the wind. She was a sophomore debater and by my senior year I was literally teaching debate to the underclassmen and riding high on the tournament circuit (winning some,) which gave me a leg up with the younger girls.

Nevertheless, as a boy I was the hero child. Expected to do great things, considered smart, and–early on–athletic. I loved sports but I was far from really being an athlete. I could get good grades all through public school without trying too hard. Early in high school, my parents decided I should be a lawyer. I had wanted to be a second baseman or a quarterback. The first day at Adamson High in Dallas, I got the shit knocked out of me on the football field, and all notions of athletic glory vanished as I opted for the debate team. Being good at debate led my mother to believe (as she did ever after) that I must be a lawyer, perhaps a politician. There was talk of the presidency; the country badly needed another great leader like FDR. Sounded good to me. Then.

I probably never should have gone to law school. It certainly was not my idea. My parents decided I should be a lawyer in 1953. It was my first year of high school and I got into the debate program at W. H. Adamson High School in Oak Cliff, a part of Dallas. Failing at athletics, too small and skinny, I had gone to the room where debaters were actually recruited by the master debate coach, Carl Nutley.

The program was one of the best in the nation. Adamson had won the national championship in 1950. It was an anomaly because Oak Cliff in those days was a blue-collar, working-class neighborhood, not the demographics of your usual hotshot debate programs, which were more likely to exist at a school like Lamar in the River Oaks section of Houston, our archrival. I know a large number of lawyers and judges in Texas because so many of the high school debaters went on to law school.

In 1952, as an eighth grader, caught up in the media image of Eisenhower as war hero, I urged–practically commanded–my parents to vote for Ike for president. When they returned from the polling place, I confronted them. They had voted for Adlai Stevenson, the politician among all I would see in my life span (I don't remember FDR) I would regard as the most intelligent and civilized ever to grace a podium. But in 1952, I was sorely disappointed in my parents for rejecting Ike.

By 1956, having seen the light, I was fervently for Stevenson, and again in 1960, when he was not even willing to run. I yearned for Stevenson and reluctantly accepted John Kennedy. By November of that year (having turned 21, the voting age then), I happily and enthusiastically cast my first vote for JFK and a New Frontier in American politics.

I remember my exact moment of enlightenment. It was at the Baylor Speech Institute held each summer for high school debaters. More than speech technique was discussed in classes. A professor from Tulane, a former Baylor debater named Cannon, talked about McCarthyism that flourished and was intimidating political dialogue, bringing on repression and suppression of dissent. He simply raised questions and lo, a process was begun: thinking. A dangerous business, that.

The universe opened up to me; books became tools that further expanded my horizons and a lifelong habit of reading started. I am grateful for this awakening. So much lay ahead.

I first got drunk at age 16 and I was off on a drinking life of 25 years, alcoholic like dad. Sometimes in later life I wondered whether I could have chosen not to drink. It seemed inevitable in retrospect. Just a matter of time and opportunity. No matter how sincere I was growing up in my vows of abstinence, I could no more decline the elixir than I could be good in math or comfortable in country clubs. It was not to be.

I first got drunk in February 1956, after a high school debate tournament we failed to win. There had been a New Year's Eve party for the senior debaters only. (I was a junior.) There was champagne left over (a fact I later would regard as incredible) and we got our hands on it. Later that night I was terribly sick. But it didn't matter, I'd found the magic elixir.

It thoroughly transformed me into a witty, gregarious, utterly charming fellow, in my view. Shyness, tentativeness, uncertainty, fear of any kind, vanished when I introduced alcohol into my body. The vast potential I thought I had for being cool became reality. For an alcoholic, the elixir does something it does not and never can for "earth people" (as non-alkies are known in the rooms of AA meetings). I remembered my solemn and, at the time, sincere promises, I had made to my mother that I would never drink. But the power of the elixir was far too potent to overcome.

Curiosity turned to compulsion early on. I couldn't drink all the time. Jesus, I was a junior in high school. After that night, anytime I could get hold of even a single beer, I eagerly quaffed it down, wanting more. It took about 25 years before I could get enough.

From There to Here

Molly is partially blind but doesn't let that stop her. Most days she and I ramble around our old house in the Clarksville neighborhood of Austin, Texas, moving from room to room, searching, resting, roaming.

My real introduction to drinking was at drive-in movies. At Southern Methodist University (SMU) in 1957 my friends and I started going to them with six-packs of cheap beer. Drinking a whole six-pack of Berghoff beer (at 89 or 99 cents) was the goal. Being underage for buying booze and either living at home (as I did) or in a campus dorm, neither of which allowed drinking, we had to have a place to guzzle our beers.

It was almost always in a car and the rite of drive-in movie drinking became a recurring one. This piker's drinking was about all that we could manage at SMU, which was almost like an extension of high school for me and most of my friends still living at home.

Sometimes there would be a party with some of the liberal professors who held forth thoughtfully and eloquently, it seemed then. The best of these was Paul Boller, a history professor who was literate, articulate and liberal. These infrequent occasions were sit-around drinking and talking sessions; so besides broadening our intellectual horizons they afforded an opportunity to further the development of alcoholism (for me).

Only one of my regular crew of buddies at SMU was also, it seems to me now, an alcoholic. Naturally, he was the friend to whom I was most drawn. The summer before I left SMU for good, Len rented a small bungalow near the campus. He actually sub-leased the place from Dr. Boller who was away for that summer. It was a place where we could all–especially Len and I–drink all we wanted in peace. Sometimes I would just sleep over, being too drunk to drive home.

There was in downtown Dallas out on Akard Street–that still had frame houses back then–a notorious whore we called Akard Annie. She was old, ugly and incredibly unappealing. For a pittance, she hoisted her dirty cotton skirt and spread her legs. You had to get in and come fast. No nonsense. And considering how she looked, you wanted to come fast and get out of the smelly, old house and as far away as possible. It was strictly a last resort for terminally horny college boys. There was a joke that no one had ever gone to Akard Annie twice. Once was enough, more than enough.

I had already had my one time with the old gargoyle when one summer night in the bungalow I told Len about her. Our loins stirred, more it seemed as we threw more empty beer bottles aside. At last he had to take his one time in the sack with the skuzzy old whore, and off we charged to Akard Street. Afterwards I mused that I had to be the only repeat customer she had ever had. At the moment of truth I had pulled out the dollar bills and then my cock and climbed on, thinking what the hell.

Getting laid and getting high were about the only pursuits that resulted in pleasure, and it seemed to me that's what one sought. I had about as little control over my sexual urges and activities as I had over booze. The conversation at the bungalow always seemed to swing back around to sex. We each had screwed whores in Mexico (where I met the sublime form of elixir, tequila, and it seemed almost psychedelic).

My friend Len who had the sacred outpost of debauchery, the bungalow near SMU, that summer was dating (and fucking) a high-powered female debater at SMU (whom I believe he later married). He was a former Lamar High debater and regarded like the "Fonz" in our small circle of friends, in other words, Mr. Cool. One steamy summer night the two of us discussed our sexual conquests, such as they were, and were not tempted to head back to Akard Street. We became more engrossed than usual with the details and got more into it than was wise considering our drunken state. Finally, Len said he bet his prick was bigger, longer, than mine, the usually implicit male challenge.

This was very surprising coming from him as he was not macho or any kind of braggart. I demurred, not caring much either way. He produced a ruler and said: let's just see. We each fished our cocks out and commenced fiddling around with measuring, trying to get an erection, whereupon he purported to help me measure mine. I then realized that he was holding it, not really trying to measure it. Like a lightning bolt I realized for the first time (I had not had a glimmer of suspicion up to this point) what was really going on.

But my member had already realized and was stiff as the discarded ruler (though not as long), responding to the touch of my best friend. I did not fight it but rather reciprocated the fondling and as we lay back, like the two ends of a Jack of Diamonds, I again thought: what the hell.

This, of course, was the watershed event of that otherwise dull summer, shocking and disturbing at some level. The result of acculturation, then so strong, was what today we know as homophobia. At times I was appalled at what we had done. How could it have happened? Neither Len nor I considered ourselves homosexual, or even bisexual, after this surprising incident.

But I was not really given in those days to worrying about what I did, especially if I had already done it. Remorse was not prominent in my panoply of emotions. Nor excessive guilt. I never reconciled it except to think, as I do now, what the hell; it was just sex. I did not then, and do not now, think there was anything morally wrong with what we did.

With other buddies in younger years I had engaged in masturbation, each to his own. Other guys at Boy Scout Camp had gone further in my presence. None of it really seemed perverted to me. Moreover, in my sunset years I have come to agree with others that it is "natural" to be attracted to individuals of both sexes. Society teaches us the revulsion (fear) of sex with our own gender; you've got to be taught. To have a preference for sex with women is not to have a repulsion or aversion to sex with men. Preference does not imply exclusivity.

The natural state is probably bisexuality but the forces of our culture drive us exclusively into one camp or the other according to what we prefer. But it is not written in stone and deviation from the "norm" is not unusual in my experience of people. (However, I have lived in the well known "Gomorrah of the Southwest" for nearly 50 years. Or, as my old friend Johnny Womack dubbed Austin, "the poor man's Alexandria".)

I can tell you this: I was not repulsed by what Len and I did. On the contrary, we both enjoyed it and we were both unnecessarily troubled by that, not wishing at all to be branded "one of them." At that time, the epithet "queer" was the most pejorative one you could be called in the culture of teen age boys. We each continued to have relationships with women and the two of us were good friends until our paths diverged.

The summer ended and I left Dallas behind, found Austin, and a whole new chapter of my life opened. I saw Len a few times after that night, in passing, and then I lost track and have not seen or heard from him in 40 years. In this episode the experience pre-dated the thinking about it. That summer at SMU I had done something without thinking about it; much later I would think about it a good deal but do nothing.

All of those SMU friends faded away and what I wind up remembering about SMU is the long hours of sitting in the Student Union playing bridge and chain-smoking Marlboros. And, the biggy: between semesters of my freshman year my father died.

In Dallas in the fall of 1957, as I started college at SMU, my mother moved out of the house we owned on Galloway in Oak Cliff, taking my sister who was finishing high school.

My sister Jackie is 15 months younger than I am. We grew up close. I teased her mercilessly but we have always (except for a few years she was in a cult) been close friends. She was helpful to my recovery in AA. As kids, especially in Waco, we went all over town together. As big brother, I looked after her and I probably still tend to see her, like in the movies, as the angelic kid sister, and I still have great affection for her.

I remained living in the house with my father. He had finally gotten sober after a stint at a sanitarium in the Oak Lawn area.

The place was grim, as they were then. No brightly lit dayrooms or lively meetings or bright counselors. You laid it out, dried out, toughed through the remorse and boredom of long idle days in the darkly lit old house. Just being there was depressing. Oppressive food smells permeated the place, along with ubiquitous cigarette smoke.

Two AA men had come to our house, perfect models of the stereotypes then of old dry drunks. For all I know they were as lively, funny and happy as the hundreds of alcoholics I would encounter a quarter century later. But in demeanor and appearance they were gray and somber with a sense of having laid waste to their brains and bodies, like alkies were if they stayed alive (quit drinking).

My dad had been sober for a short time when my mother left. As far as I know he stayed that way until I found his body on New Year's Day 1958. There were empty prescription drug bottles in the room. Had he taken them? What drugs were they? We would never know but in my heart I felt he had done it.

There was a populist Justice of the Peace in Oak Cliff who knew full well that life insurance companies would not pay benefits to the family if death was a suicide. He nixed an autopsy and wrote that death was due to a coronary occlusion. We got the small insurance benefit.

I saw this happen and later I came to know the reputation of Judge W.E. Richberg. I thought I, alone maybe, knew the truth about my dad. I am not 100 percent sure about it now. I still believe it was likely suicide. Perhaps, as his older brother, my uncle A.D. would later suggest to me, he had kept reaching for the medication until he accidentally took too much. Unless there is a hereafter, which I have no reason to believe, it will remain an enigma.

It scared me to find my father dead in his bed that New Year's Day. I had slept very late in the house with my father's corpse for at least 4 or 5 hours. I knew instantly when I woke that things were not right. The house was quiet, too quiet.

When I thought about how he was after my mother left, how bleak the future seemed to him, I could not really imagine him going on–being alive. I could not see how it could end other than the way it did. He was gone and I would never again experience life the same way I had for the 18 years before.

I don't remember going to any funerals between my Aunt Ruth's in 1947 and my dad's in 1958. Each of them affected me strongly, from my first awareness of death to the proof that it could take away my dearest family member in an instant, or over the agonizingly slow voyage my mother's life ended with.

Even after Aunt Ruth's funeral in Cleburne it was not my dad I feared would die. By the time he died, I knew he wanted to. Early sobriety, I learned in my adulthood, was a rocky, rocky time. My Dad simply lost any will to live. To be there with him watching him crumble made me feel he was pathetic. I vowed I would never be that way, and in a sense, it has kept me from too much dependency on the women I have loved; but has it also kept me from giving myself completely?

My deepest fear growing up had been that my mother would die. I was a junior in high school in 1956 when I went early to a debate tournament in Muskogee, Oklahoma to be part of a new contest. I took the train from the old train station in Dallas. I was to stay with the family of a Muskogee High School debater. His father turned out to be a mortician, the funeral parlor being below their second floor living quarters. The idea of being in the same building with a few cadavers, along with the insecurity of traveling alone (instead of on the chartered bus with the whole squad), kept me awake all night that night.

My greatest vulnerability appeared in the form of fear of death, particularly the fear of my mother's death. I depended on her in a deeply strategic way that I did not depend upon my dad.

I loved him; he was easy to love, endearing, sort of hapless. He had artistic talent and had come close to being employed at Walt Disney in California in 1937. He really should have been a fine artist, painting and living with his work and without so much responsibility. I will remember my whole life going to the ballgames he took me to and fishing the rivers around Waco and his telling jokes to Stubby the dog. I also always remember sitting up late into the night on weekends listening to him spin the dreams he lived on.

I knew it was the booze talking, but how I wanted to believe it could be the way he saw it in his imagination. I cannot recall now what the substance of his dreams was, but always it involved him triumphantly overcoming present hardship in some glorious endeavor. When he passed out, I carried him to his bed like you carry a child, grateful there would not be any fighting on that night.

My dad Marcus had been the youngest of five children. My Irish grandmother had babied him unabashedly into adulthood. She called him Markie. In fact everyone in the family had the "ee" sound added to their name by her. My mother was Stellie, my uncle John Henry was Hennie. Some of us were naturals, me, Jimmy; my sister, Jackie; my (favorite) aunt, Addie.

It seemed my dad had simply come into the world as a person everyone loved, good looking to a fault, the prize child of his family, but lacking the coping skills necessary to survive. Although neither of my paternal grandparents even drank at all, Markie was a born alcoholic. He never had a choice. The elixir had him in its magic power from first taste, just as it did me.

There was alcoholism, the "Irish virus," all through our family on both sides, except that none of my four grandparents ever touched a drop. Like others, I loved my father, but I had to look out for him, not vice versa. The strength I leaned on was my mother's. Without her, I dare not say what would have become of me.

I have complained long and loud that my parents had my vocation set long before I left high school. I had to be a lawyer. But at least they stressed education and thereby gave me a chance to be better than I would have been and to do better in the world than they did.

Poverty and constant struggle were an integral part of life for all their lives. By pushing me into college and beyond, they pushed me out of that zone of desperation they had always inhabited. While lawyering certainly did not make me rich, it did spare me from poverty.

The warm fuzzy memories of growing up in Waco had given me the idea I wanted to go to Baylor. With my dad taking me to Baylor Bear games and my fantasies of growing up to be quarterback of the team, it was inevitable that someday, somehow I would matriculate at the Baptist university in Waco.

By the time I did, it was clear I was not going to be on the football team at all. Debate got me to Baylor. I had had a modest scholarship at SMU that only covered tuition, so I could manage to go there if I lived at home. To go away to school I needed a real scholarship. The inimitable Professor Glenn Capp, debate coach at Baylor, provided me with a full scholarship that paid almost everything except a beer allowance.

Prof Capp, as he was universally known, was perhaps the premier college debate coach of the '50s and '60s. His teams won many honors. You would never guess that he was the top man in his field from his presence or demeanor. He was a quiet, gentle soul, who exerted strong leadership in an almost imperceptible way. His instincts were true and he was a man of principle, being one of the three liberals on the faculty at Baylor University in 1958. He did so much for so many. In my case, he made my boyhood dream of going to Baylor come true, though he knew nothing of that dream or my Waco background.

Going to Baylor in the '50s was like being in the Marine Corps. Afterwards you always remember the experience nostalgically and you have some great stories to tell, but the living of it in real time is miserable. So

Baylor, after the comparatively liberal and sophisticated SMU, was like being in a Baptist concentration camp. Dancing was prohibited on campus, which was exemplary of the strictness, but no imposition on me.

There was, as I found out the hard way, out-and-out censorship of the student newspaper. When as a sophomore journalism student I wrote an editorial in favor of integration that slipped by and was published, a hand written directive from the President of the university to the Lariat editor put an end to all editorials on the subject of integration. Baylor was all-white, 99 percent Baptist (it seemed,) conservative as only fundamentalists can be.

I was a babe in wonderland, or a kind of totally alien world of cretins. Insanity seemed imminent until I met one of only three (counting me) enlightened students at BU. I lived in Room 306 at the ancient Brooks Hall dorm. Pete Jones also lived elsewhere in the cavernous dorm and was suffering worse culture shock than I was. He had transferred from Yale. We both espoused agnosticism and shared an abiding love of spirits, the bottled kind.

Soon, when my first roommate was expelled for clobbering an Aggie, Pete moved into my room and along with Wacoan George Schell–a fellow debater and a guy I had known since first grade at Provident Heights–constituted the civilized contingent at Baylor. They were my only two friends.

Pete and I were nearly expelled the first week for drunkenness. The hearsay nature of the evidence (an unidentified snitch) barely saved us.

Chapel for two years was required to graduate from Baylor. I never darkened the door of the twice a week services. But Pete, George and I did participate in religious activity. Out on the Bosque River the Coca Cola company had a modest camp they had either abandoned or used rarely. We took adverse possession of it as an ideal site for our temple (and great place to drink beer). Our very own church was dubbed the Lord's Church of Fire.

On Sunday evening when no meal was served at the cafeteria on campus, we repaired to the camp, built a large fire outside, roasted hotdogs over the roaring fire, and drank large quantities of beer, which brought on the Holy Spirit. There was preaching, gospel singing and plain old howling–the three of us carrying on into the night, building the fire up, chugging beers, all but speaking in tongues in our irreverent and doubtlessly blasphemous worship. I have never before or since enjoyed religious activities so much.

Luckily, river residents who surely could hear our fervor never snitched on us. Religious freedom carried the day on the Bosque, if not at Baylor. Or maybe they thought they were hearing services at some real church.

Someone I remember with no small nostalgia is the SMU coed named Caroline who really fits into the "Baylor era." (I remember Len, too, and wonder what happened to him.)

The summer before going to Baylor I met a beautiful SMU art student, Caroline Gerdes, blonde in the way Marilyn Monroe was (but natural) and physically as well endowed. I can't remember where I met her exactly. My friends all said she was too pretty for me and surely, she was.

At Baylor I lived for the weekends I could get home to Dallas and Caroline. The deacons of the Lord's Church of Fire were properly impressed based on a large photograph of Caroline I kept on the pathetic desk in our barren dorm room. When I returned from Dallas weekends, I was misty and distracted. The deacons knew why and waited patiently for Sunday and the rousing services we would conduct on the banks of the Bosque.

Something happened with Caroline when I moved back to Dallas. I think it was my fault; she slipped away, and I don't think that was the way she wanted it. At the tender age, all the girls and women I liked or loved and spent time with, from Sherry to Helen (whom I married), were important to my dawning adulthood but I truly regret the loss of the beautiful Caroline by virtue of the way I was with her.

She was sensitive; I was too often insensitive and caught up with the competitive and conspiratorial camaraderie of my running buddies. She deserved a lot better and I'm confident she found that later with someone worthy of her. The thought of her kept me going at Baylor. That and the Lord's Church of Fire. My comeuppance was waiting for me to meet a zany Jewish girl at SMU and have my heart really broken.

SMU had a patina of liberalism (largely due to the Perkins School of Theology) and sophistication. At its core the school was a fairly decent if unexciting regional university. Baylor was then a provincial, narrow-minded college that never transcended the town of Waco. I had loved Waco as a boy of 10. Nine years later Waco was nearly unbearable. Debate scholarship and Lord's Church of Fire notwithstanding, I had to leave Baylor behind.

I took Chemistry in summer school at SMU because I thought it would be easier than at UT in the massive required courses. However, as it happened, my chemistry lab partner Leslie and I developed so much chemistry we could not do our assignments. I can't even think back on this girl without again feeling the desperate want I had for her for a full year, even long after I last saw her. She had hit a chord with me and it set off a music I could not control or shut off.

She was Jewish–not the child of urban intellectuals (for whom I have so much admiration) but of suburban merchants, well heeled and upwardly mobile, in the parlance of the time. She was in rebellion against the observant parents, conservative bourgeoisie that they truly were. I was in rebellion against all things boring. Going to SMU, she lived at home where her parents could almost control her.

She was a slight, disheveled girl who wore glasses on her thin face. She was the antithesis of glamour (SMU had plenty of that) but she was attractive in an unconventional way and I liked her looks. She obviously was at a place in her life where she did not give a shit about much of anything. That may have been what attracted me so much to her. We became partners in crime, atheists among the Methodists.

From the first let-loose "French kiss", I yearned for her in a way I never had for any girl. We drank booze together, ran wild (as the Methodists would say,) and made clumsy teenage love in the backseat of my mother's Chevrolet or on blankets under the stars at White Rock Lake.

I was into Josh White back then; I had at least one album that I'm pretty sure I left at Leslie's house. In Austin I was wont to take whoever I could to the New Orleans Club on Red River and listen to the incomparable pianist/singer Ernie Mae Miller do "Saint James Infirmary," a lot like Josh White's version.

I couldn't get enough of the wildness Leslie and I created together and I was conscious that the odds of winning this girl were long. I was from Oak Cliff and the wrong faith, though I actually had none and would have converted gladly. I went through a period then of loving all things Jewish. I had Chagall prints in my room. I could have been an honorary Zionist. I would have submitted to circumcision 20 years after birth if I could have won Leslie.

Before Leslie I had had sexual experience with maybe a half dozen girls in high school and at college, as well as a few prostitutes in La Grange (near Austin,) Fort Worth and Mexico. (I don't even count Akard Annie in Dallas.) Yet it seems to me now I knew very little about sex. I knew I liked it, not a whole lot more. The connection between Leslie and me was not primarily sexual. That was something we did fairly badly, to be wild, and feed our self-image as bohemian rebels, bad to the bone.

But there was still a strong sexual attraction. Kissing each other was the best contact we had. We melded the wetness of our mouths, lips and tongues for long passionate moments. Would this necking and petting have developed into a more mature and satisfying sexual union if we had stayed together? I will never know. Even now, the voice of the romantic naïf I was is saying yes. With regard to actual coitus, we did it in short bursts of sexual energy, only in the missionary position.

But we valued each other as partners against a fucked-up world, sort of like Holden Caulfield with a sexy buddy. I believed whole-heartedly that I was in love with her and 45 years later, I can't say with conviction that I was not. I don't know why this unlikely, crazy girl so completely captured my imagination, causing the hardest fall of my young life when, inevitably it did not work out.

As it was, it was only a summer romance cut short by her parents sending her to California to visit relatives, as they succeeded in the bigger objective of dispatching from her the bad influence goy. I had lost Caroline out of self-centered neglect and indifference. But I danced all my attendance on Leslie, when we could be together, and I would have married her in an instant. One of the last times I saw her was probably in the late fall of 1960. We were driving in my mother's car in Dallas and I said: let's keep driving south back to Austin and get married now. She said: Okay. We got out to Oak Cliff before we both realized we could not do it.

How could I have seriously considered shanghaiing my mother's sole transportation to run away with this girl I barely knew (but might have loved)? Since then I have reflected on our bright-burning, short-lived love and I am glad we did not try to take it further. We were not suited as mates if we had to live in the real world and where else is there in the end to live? Besides if I had been with Leslie, as I longed to be, I might not have met Nancy, the real and only love of my life. Leslie is only a short story, more than a footnote, but of course she's the girl I will never quite forget.

Old Austin

I have a tiny law office on the "main street of Clarksville," a neighborhood descended from the Reconstruction era community of the same name. Started by freed slaves. Black families, perhaps some descendants of the freed slaves, still live here, but it is a multi-racial neighborhood. My real office is in my 80-year-old bungalow style house here in the 'ville. My only legal help is Molly, the small, black poodle mix.

The University of Texas at Austin was what I had been looking for as I sojourned south on Interstate 35. I loved it from the first day in August 1959. Soon I would deplore having to return to Dallas at all and, after the summer of 1960 with Leslie, I never did really return to Dallas for more than a weekend. I left it behind.

For me college was a progression south on I-35, starting at SMU in Dallas, transferring to Baylor University in Waco on full debate scholarship, finally to Austin and the University of Texas. Arriving in Austin in August of 1959, I was home. For the next 20 years, Austin was the finest place on the planet to live. By spring of the first year, I was hopelessly in love with the town.

I had no car and very little money. In fact, if I had not gotten a job as grader/assistant to a philosophy professor, I could not have enrolled in the spring of 1960. The $50 a month barely put me over the top. At that time, poor people–students and slackers–could subsist in Austin for almost nothing. There was abundant cheap housing available around UT and elsewhere. The cost of living was low. Blue plate specials could be had at Slick's, San Jack Cafe, Galloway's or Hillsberg's for 50 to 75 cents. A haircut was 50 cents at the barber college on East 6th, long before it was the French Quarter of Austin, the swinging nightlife scene. Back then there were only Hispanic bars, blaring loud music into the street but empty inside. Good clothes could be purchased at Goodwill for pennies. Sitting at a large communal table out in Scholz' beer garden one could drink from pitchers that always sat on the table. Manna from heaven.

Austin was heaven. In 1959 when I first came to live there in the old leftist Guild Cooperative, there was no traffic, no lines at restaurants, no rude people, no hassles. There were 160,000 inhabitants! Eccentricity still flourished, from Bicycle Annie to the Beat Generation remnants. Folk legends sprang up around the eccentrics. It was not a self-conscious thing; no one would have used the word eccentric.

Bicycle Annie, who had been known as the Indian Princess, walked all over Austin pushing her bicycle with various bags attached to it. She reportedly sold subscriptions to a newspaper long since folded, if it ever existed. She sometimes had physical difficulty, but anyone who sought to help her earned her wrath. She was Austin proud.

Sarah, who presided over the Dry Creek beer joint near Mount Bonnell, was similarly independent and proud. She was famous for her surliness to customers, particularly the fraternity boys from UT, whom she seemed to despise. The Dry Creek was a very rundown ramshackle place with an upstairs sort of porch facing west so you could bask in gold and violet sunsets over Lake Austin. Best of all, the old jukebox had Tex Ritter's "Hillbilly Heaven" on it, three plays for a quarter. When we weren't at the preferred Bull Creek Lodge, Nancy and I were sometimes at Sarah's place, punching in repeated plays of "Hillbilly Heaven," downing endless bottles of cold Pearl Beer, staring out over the placid waters of the narrow channel of Lake Austin.

The lakes, Austin and Travis, were my retreat, my sanctuary, my place of choice in those years (but not in 25 years now). To hit the winding roads out of town overlooking the hilly banks of the lake with strategically staked beer sources was to escape care and hassle and to set the spirit free to soar. I knew all the spots, both natural (like Windy Point before there was a "hippie hollow") and man-made oases (like Three Points, Hi-Line Marina, Five Points).

Life was good in Austin, magical; the entire zone was comfortable. I've never had a deeper sense of freedom, of the vast possibilities of life. Freedom from the ubiquitous materialism of this culture. The potential for life–really living–was everywhere in whispered promises. I was 19 years old and turned on by a city full of all the things I liked.

I turned 21 the day before I voted for the first time, in the Democratic primary, then later for JFK for president in a big campaign of hope and new beginnings. The action had been mainly in the Young Democrats but I also joined the student chapter of Americans for Democratic Action and Young Peoples Socialist League. To be on a college campus that even had these groups was immensely exciting.

I briefly dated an intelligent and lovely girl named Doris in the spring of 1960. Our problem was that there were so few places we could go together because she was black and most places like the movies, the bars, the restaurants were still segregated.

We were both officers in the UTYD's and once after a meeting we had gone in a group to Scholz'. Out in the beer garden the waitress said she could not serve Doris and she could not remain in the place. Thinking quickly somebody said, she's Cuban, not Negro. And we used our Spanish to talk with her. She had fairly light skin so she was served but only because she was "Cuban." This illustrated how ridiculous the policy was, but it was something she did not want to have to do a lot–risking greater humiliation if the ruse was uncovered. Together we went to remote spots on Lake Travis, or sat around my apartment listening to music during quiet evenings when my voluble roommate was out. Many students went on dates to the movies, not us.

The war in Viet Nam was history waiting to happen. But by the fall of 1960 it seemed possible to have a different kind of government that would serve the people and seek peace. Hope was alive in America. I had become very active in the Young Democrats, being President of the University of Texas YD's and later holding statewide office. The assassinations of the '60s and the war in Viet Nam led me away from electoral politics.

In the summer of 1961, an ad hoc group began to demonstrate at local movie theaters starting with the Texas and Varsity on the Drag in an attempt to desegregate them. We called these actions stand-ins. Everybody lined up in front of the ticket booth as though to buy tickets for the show. When you reached the window you said something like: I'd like a ticket IF you are selling tickets to ALL Americans regardless of race. Of course they were not. So you simply went to the back of the line and went through again so that there was a perpetual line tying up the ticket window.

It was actually the first time I had been on a picket line or in a demonstration and it would establish a life-long participation in such actions. There were a few hundred of us on most evenings. The stand-ins went on for months and in the end resulted in integration at the movies, including the Paramount and State theaters downtown on Congress Avenue. I believe that in 1961 there was only one other theater, the Austin on South Congress, and three or four drive-in movies.

Our success in this direct action was sweet and fueled new efforts in coming years. After a stand-in we would gather and sing old labor songs from the Wobbly red songbook, frequently at Houston Wade's house. While there was no organizational structure, Houston chaired most meetings held at the old Y at Guadalupe and 22nd Streets. Later, my friend Vivian Franklin told me of a meeting of student activists to be held at Port Huron, Michigan, out of which came Students for a Democratic Society. I wish I had gone.

In September 1961, right after Hurricane Carla struck the Texas coast, I met a very unusual person at Threadgill's original gas-station honky-tonk out on North Lamar owned by the legendary singer, picker and yodeler, Kenneth Threadgill. Janis Joplin could have been there that night; I don't remember.

It was my final semester of Arts and Sciences after I temporarily (as it turned out) fled law school in the spring of that year. I was not trying too hard at college, sort of tumbling along in great abandon, uncertain of what I would do, drinking. I lived in a dump, a room in a "private dorm," so-called, but known to all tenants as the Black Hole of Calcutta. I shared a small room with an amusing psycho named David Cain. It was very cheap to live there.

One block away on the Drag was a bar where everyone I knew drank. Every day. I had a tab, which I paid occasionally if I could. The guys who owned the Bronze Door had great empathy for a man's need for unlimited beer. My flow was unlimited. I can't recall ever going to classes but I must have since I passed all courses with at least C's. Somehow.

Early in the fall semester I went to Threadgill's for live music one night and met Helen Read. She was unlike anyone else I had ever met, in a good way. She was very shy, so soft-spoken it was hard to tell what she said. One thing appealing to me as a self-conscious intellectual (perhaps in my mind only) was the fact that she wrote poetry. She had come to the University with her sister from Corpus Christi and like me and all my friends they had no money. Everyone I knew was destitute yet we all got by.

Having a tab for life's chief necessity was helpful. Throughout all the years I drank, starting with 1959 when I really lived on my own for the first time, I felt little need to eat. So I spent little on food. With my narrow, jail-like room costing $17.50 per month, and a tab for beer, I hardly needed any money. Helen had a true genius for living on nothing. She had grown up really poor, poorer than my family. We perceived ourselves as intellectuals and bohemians who were from poor working-class families. Our politics and world-view was pretty much the same. And all our time was spent amidst people like ourselves.

Although in retrospect it still seems unlikely, we wound up together that first night in a cramped back bedroom of a cheap shotgun apartment that had been passed around in our circle of friends. I'd lived there with two roommates the summer before. In the upstairs apartment, a group called The Hogs was involved in their annual ritual, which entailed the sacrifice of a real armadillo. (The people nowadays who talk about keeping Austin weird, well. . . they have no idea.)

I can still remember walking the eight or ten blocks from the apartment to the Black Hole of Calcutta in the early first light of dawn. Before that time I had never been conscious of making love to a virgin before. It could have happened, certainly my high school girlfriends Sherry and Allison, professed virginity. The first time with Helen was more notable for its novelty than for pleasure. She was very tight and the experience left my penis sore. It was curiously satisfying however.

The tryst was to be repeated night after night as we independently went to the same places and wound up together, me walking back to my cell in the first light. I know now that back then, at 22, I knew so little about sex as together Helen and I learned some things, she the true virgin (at 22) and I the experienced unlearned one.

In the spring we moved in together in a small but easily domesticated apartment on the east side of campus. Helen had one thing that was very precious in Austin then–a job. I think she worked only part-time until the spring semester, and then I can't recall her going to classes, only working at the University of Texas Press as a proofreader. I gave up the Bronze Door, which shortly failed, probably due to the tab system for so many alcoholics.

I did the unthinkable. I went back to law school in spring 1962, when I could see no real alternative. I did not want to leave the University and I felt I could not tolerate grad school in either English or Philosophy, my double major in undergraduate school. Thus, I split my first year of law school with a whole year between the first and second semesters. I was back at Townes Hall among the many former debaters I knew, reading cases.

That summer I read Harper Lee's "To Kill a Mockingbird" and it reminded me of past summers when I had read endlessly about Clarence Darrow and become inspired by what I could do as a lawyer. I thought I saw a way to be a lawyer that I could tolerate, even love. Quickly, almost imperceptibly, we slipped into the familiar pattern of law students–man going to law school with his woman working to support them. I still had some resources but soon it was Helen who supported us.

We had started as self-conscious bohemians with literary aspirations in what we saw as a Henry Miller type scene, the nether side of Austin I immediately loved. We metamorphosed into the law school couple syndrome without ever intending to or talking about it.

However, we were not typical. My sole act of establishing and trying to maintain my difference was to put up a sign saying: "I am among you, but not of you", intended for the law school. My attendance was so irregular I could have gotten a visitor's parking permit.

In summer, I accepted an offer from my uncle A.D., my dad's older brother, to go to Phoenix and work in his sign painting business. He had started helping me financially during the prior spring. He knew I was struggling to go to law school. A loan here, a small job there.

I was entirely unprepared for what I found in the middle-class suburbs of Tempe, Arizona in that hot summer of 1962. I stayed in the guest bedroom of my uncle and aunt's house, which meant no privacy, no way to get away except to work. And what work it was.

Assisting a professional sign painter, my uncle's employees, out in the desert painting billboards in 120 degrees heat. No opportunity to drink except on weekends when I could get buses into Phoenix. My uncle was a recovered alcoholic sober through AA and I didn't think much of that, even though I had seen how alcohol killed my own father. I had yet to get on the express train to the bottom myself. They were so Republican and conservative that the periodicals that came for me led my aunt to say I must be a Communist.

I lasted maybe three weeks and I invested about all I had earned in an airplane ticket to Austin where I would arrive with no place to live, no money and no idea what to do with myself. So I knew it would be fine. Austin was a safe harbor of personal freedom and I couldn't get back soon enough.

Among passengers boarding the plane in El Paso was Sam Houston Clinton, Jr., a labor lawyer and friend from the Young Democrats. When we landed in Austin Sam offered me a ride; he had left his car at the airport. There was no talk of where we would go, where to take me or the like as we drove straight to Scholz' Garden and its big friendly arms opened to me. I was home again.

I linked up with other Austin friends who put me up. I managed to get beer. I had really missed Helen and I found her quickly. There is a crowd of what I have always called Old Austin, good friends and interesting, eccentric people whose individuality was the glue holding us together within a society we collectively found too materialistic, religious and inhibiting to the spirit.

These were people we met back in the first couple of years at UT: John Womack, who worked at the UT Main Library and painted landscapes of the Texas Hill Country, was one of the more stable of these friends. When he died in 2004 he was retired from the library after 50 years; he had lived a gentle life, much loved by friends. James Gardner, a true bearded Beatnik figure on campus, where he worked in the Chemistry Department for many years, had been married to Gwen, whom I had met in the Young Democrats. Ran Moran, ever the political activist, and a man whose principles have stayed in place over decades of living in Manhattan and Austin. Bill and Jean Fowler, devout progressives, themselves well grounded; they were always gracious to friends down and out from drink or just from being cultural outsiders. Then there were the likes of David Dean, Pat Thornton, Horace Johnson, so many of these old Austinites we partied with and supported and were supported by in those early years and for all the years. Few survive today.

Of course, I can't omit my good friend Tom Johnson, who was probably the most alcoholic of the people I knew, and that's saying something. Perhaps he would have said the same about me. Ironically, we both sobered up at about the same time but far apart, each of us thinking that surely the other had died of the grape; we were glad to find each other again, and sober, in the early '90s.

Until his death in 1999 he was on my short list of people I loved to just sit and converse with, which we did as often as we could. Once in a dingy deli near campus we had come to an epiphany that the failure of our country and capitalist culture had started with the move of the Brooklyn Dodgers out of Brooklyn to Los Angeles. If there is a heaven, it will be filled with the kind of unconventional folk we found living in the Old Austin of the late fifties and sixties.

Helen was very afraid her father would find out we were living together in sin. I really wanted the peaceful domestic scene we had shared in the spring. Somehow, the subject of marriage came up but it was not broached by me. My own parents had split up just weeks before my dad died. I had seen what family responsibilities had done to crush his artistic impulses and circumscribe his life in a way he could not live with. I had no attraction to the idea of being married and I still fancied myself a non-conformist, an intellectual bohemian, sort of a hitch-hiker on the road with the Beat Generation. I scornfully eschewed the middle-class lifestyle. Being in my uncle's suburban Arizona home for three weeks had not endeared mainstream America to me.

I loved Helen (as I believe most who knew her did), but I hardly wanted any permanent situation. Precisely because the institution of marriage meant so little to me, I agreed to cloak our comfortable relationship with its protection from the certainty of death by shotgun if old man Read discovered us. I figured hey, it's only a legal thing, no big deal. Marriages were entered and exited all the time.

I wanted to live with Helen who was a remarkable person with a tremendous capacity to empathize with others. She was deeply compassionate and kind. I had never known anyone with such soft but insightful sensibilities.

We shared our values right down the line. Besides drinking and making love, we spent a lot of time in the stand-ins to integrate movie theaters that first fall together. On things political, in which I deeply believed, we agreed. She was very intelligent without being at all pretentious. The poems she wrote were beautiful, haunting and compelling.

We loved to drink wine and just sit listening to rain falling on an afternoon. It was very comfortable just to be with Helen; I never doubted her love for me. Early on we had great fun together living in the weird fringe of Austin society.

Later, in what turned out to be a decade of marriage, we forgot to keep the fun in our lives, or we couldn't. The pressures of life put stress on a relationship not well suited for marriage to begin with. Almost immediately after our 15-minute ceremony at old Justice of the Peace Frank McBee's house in South Austin, she got pregnant. Another unplanned development.

We were playing it by ear that summer of 1962. How can I regret it when my beautiful daughter was born because all these things happened? On March 22, 1963, Eleanor Estelle Simons was born at St. David's Hospital. We had named her after Eleanor Roosevelt and my mother, Estelle. I never knew before she was born how extremely strong is the feeling of love a parent has for a child. She became the light of my life which was so often dark during those ten years.

Nancy

Molly lies comfortably near my cluttered desk and she wants to hear the story of Nancy and me, which happens to be my favorite story.

I wanted this woman.

I knew it when I first saw her at an artist's enclave at San Jacinto and 18th Streets, near Scholz' Bier Garten. She had longish dark hair, big beautiful brown eyes, dark skin, a thin beautiful body. The picture corresponded to some ideal I had back in my mind of my Zelda. (I had been reading Fitzgerald.) I saw in those gorgeous eyes the reckless quality, the longing to fly, the sensuousness. She was the woman I had looked for all my life and given up on finding when I married the year before.

I was 24 and married. I had compromised what I really yearned for in life in many ways. When I saw Nancy many doors opened in my head; I saw heights and flashes only dimly imagined before that June evening in 1963. I wanted magic and here it was. If only I could contrive some way to grasp her to me. I could not walk resignedly away simply because I was already married.

There was a dark fragrant mystery about this 22-year-old art student. Her hair always smelled like carnations, fresh and subtly aromatic. Her breath always like a sweet burnt orange. The kisses I could get always left me craving more.

It was a succulent June night at the artist colony of small apartments and I felt that finally I knew what I wanted. At the art colony at a party, we danced and I cajoled her phone number. Being totally captivated, I knew I would never get the images, the sweet smells and touch of her out of my head. But I was troubled by the fact that elsewhere in Austin that night I had a wife I cared for and an infant daughter I loved.

Two weeks or so later I called Nancy and we went out, she still not imagining that I was married. Getting to her tiny apartment, we talked shyly but cool, as we knew we should be. Her place had a smell familiar to me, paint. It evoked the smell of my father's shed and the jobs I'd gone with him on. Nancy was a painter, but an artist; she majored in painting at the UT School of Fine Arts.

We only went to a bar, of course, one called The Carousel Lounge out off Cameron Road. It was enchanting as I saw in her beautiful dark eyes all the unconventional and fiery depth my soul sought. We wanted to fly together. Instead, we stopped my ancient '49 DeSoto on Duval and danced in the street to the musical strains of the car radio. The moon was approvingly bright overhead. Life was wonderful except for the impossible situation I now had myself in. I was already in love with Nancy, but I was married to Helen and we had a beautiful little girl we called Pooh.

During the next two years, the conflict would nearly kill all of us except Pooh, who was only a baby unaware of the mess our lives were in. This was summer 1963; I was finally divorced in 1972 from Helen (an innocent party in all of this and a fine person undeserving of the hurt that came to her).

Nancy and I made love, sort of, for the first time that June night. I was too drunk to do it right. I tore my boxer shorts in two, trying to get them on or off, I don't know which. The evening ended in a haze of the booze; we quarreled in the driveway as I left. She threw gravel at me after I had insulted her because I took her for someone quite different, maybe in an effort to convince myself it would not work between us. I believed my dalliance was over. In fact, I wanted to convince myself that it was no idyllic, perfect love. In the next decade, we would repeat our soaring times and our fighting times.

It was a few nights later that we decided to run off together to New Orleans, land of dreams. We left Austin in Nancy's Chevy Impala at midnight or later. We found ourselves in Houston at the cruel onset of dawn, the idea of New Orleans not quite so appealing in morning's light. We went to my old high school and college chum's apartment on W. Alabama. George Dixie was tying his tie preparing to head off to work at his law office. Mostly, we told him, we just wanted to sleep a few hours. So after he left we hit George's bed.

I think we both knew we were going to make love, sober. All my senses were engaged by her smooth body as we made love that morning in Houston for the first time. I remember that her panties were even exotic, some pattern of colors I never knew they made panties in. I had the pleasure of removing them. Her dark skin on the white sheets, lovely medium-sized breasts–I liked what I saw and felt. We both came convulsively together as we would later do so often. Our bodies seemed to fit together as though that was the plan.

Afterwards we slept peacefully before starting back to Austin with a box of soda crackers and a bottle of champagne. I thought foolishly that if we just did it–made love–then I would get her out of my mind. But it only made it worse; I never wanted to let go. I don't know exactly what Nancy was feeling but it seemed to be close to what I felt. We wanted to go on seeing each other.

The drinking was heavy, but not alcoholic, from the start. The elixir seemed to sweep us to Dionysian heights we had only imagined. It would not always be that way.

That summer I moved out from the place Helen and I lived in the east campus area; Eleanor was only 3 months old. I took what in New York would be called a cold water flat next door to Nancy's basement apartment. We idled away many summer days listening to Pete Seeger records, swigging on imported beers or domestic wines, tenderly, exploringly making love. Evenings we made love more fervently, swept along on tides of feeling by the gin river, listening to Martin Denny's "A Taste of Honey".

By this time, Nancy knew I was married. Like me, she was helpless to stop what was happening to us. Now it wasn't just me who was troubled by the way things were. We both were and I know Helen was very unhappy. I vacillated between going stoically on with my marriage and chucking it and embracing the intense feelings I had for Nancy. Always in my thoughts was my tiny blond daughter, truly an innocent in what her father had wrought.

I first told Nancy I was married at the old Rome Inn on 29th Street, quoting lines from T.S. Eliot with a melodramatic resignation aided by a basket bottle of Chianti. I came on too strong but I was hoping she would not just get up and walk out; I could not have blamed her if she had. She accepted my promise to end a marriage I couldn't allow to keep us apart.

It's not that I was so unhappy before we met; it's just that I had not glimpsed the full flush of feelings that emerged. I hated to hurt Helen but mostly I deeply feared losing my infant daughter whom I already loved very much. I alternated between the wild heights of playing, loving and imagining our life if Nancy and I could only be together, and lows of guilt, fear and misgivings when I would dutifully resolve to stick it out, do the right thing. Also, I was in law school. That was completely beside the point.

On long hot afternoons of the second summer, Nancy and I went to Bull Creek Lodge to drink beer and swim. Music followed us around. At the funky old Bull Creek Lodge we heard a song that told us our day will come, we will sing in the sunshine. It had to be prophetic.

We were still stealing love; I had not been able to file for divorce. That did not diminish the thrill and rippling pleasure of lovemaking. In the water at Bull Creek Lodge, in the car, at Hancock Recreation Center on the golf course–wherever we could do it and not run too great a risk of arrest. Sometimes we started out to class or to a movie and before we could get there we became so beset by desire that we returned to a room, an apartment, wherever we could be rid of clothes and indulge pleasure. A hiding place by the lake would do, and did many times. We both still remember a time at Windy Point on Lake Travis.

Once we rented a canoe on Lake Austin and had to stop, go ashore in bushes to still the aching need to join our bodies. I exploded into her. That was when I believe she got pregnant. A complication that rendered our difficult situation impossible. Even so, we wanted our baby. We wanted him in the deepest way one can want something until the end when he was carried away from Nancy's outstretched arms at Baylor Hospital in Dallas, forever lost to us.

We only had ourselves to blame for that immeasurable loss, me more than her because I could not summon the will and courage to carry out the divorce. Nancy felt she was in no position to undertake raising the child unless we were bound together. We each had a child already, but we were destined not to have one together. I think about that more than ever in these later years and the growing disappointment is only bearable because we have each other.

When Lee Harvey Oswald, if it was he, shot JFK, I was living with Helen and Pooh in a house off Manor Road near Airport Blvd. Nancy's parents, knowing what was going on–to some extent anyway–insisted she live in approved student housing which in those days meant curfew, "house mother" on premises, rules. They installed her in a room of a large beautiful old house on Congress Avenue north of the Capitol around 15th Street. Still we could not cease loving, touching, lying to others, to allow it to continue.

In that fall, I rented a tiny rear apartment on W. 41st at Guadalupe for the lordly sum of $22.50 per month. It was our love nest, site of the most sensuous and secret lovemaking, ominously across from the state mental hospital.

During that school year, we found even new rarefied pinnacles of pleasure as together we learned and perfected all the various delicious ways to make love. If it was possible, we did it. If it was very pleasurable, we did it well and often. Sometimes for hours at a time. Before we had the little place for our trysts, we went to the Mount Vernon Motel in the Delwood Shopping Center which we euphemistically called "George and Martha's Place." It cost $8.00 a night and was a nice but not luxurious place. Long, slow, changing positions until you couldn't hold back anymore and you came like a volcano erupting. And erupting and . . . . Sometimes the emotion generated left her crying from pleasure, or me with my heart beating lickety split, no pun intended, so aroused we had to immediately do it again.

The great canoe outing was late in spring 1964, just before Nancy graduated with a BFA in painting from UT. She had to go home to Fort Worth after school ended. She was with child.

I had been scheduled to finish law school then. I dropped two courses to put in time for a liberal Democrat running for governor. I lacked six or eight hours having the bachelor of laws degree. Yet, I had enough hours under the rules then to take the bar exam. I was scheduled to start it one hot morning in July. Waking to that prospect, I decided it would be a good day to go to San Francisco with Nancy.

In my youth I always felt that no problem was too big to run away from. A petition for divorce had been filed by Helen; Nancy was pregnant. We needed to escape. Drastic measures were called for, were they not? We set out in my green 1955 Mercury with good tires to drive into a brand new life in The City by the Bay.

We followed old Route 66 it seemed. Stayed in Tucumcari, Flagstaff, Las Vegas, San Luis Obispo. Arriving in the Bay Area, somehow we went straight to Berkeley. We sat in a place called LaVal's, near the UC campus, staring at classified ads for apartments–cheap apartments. I have always gravitated towards college campuses. I feel at home there. I liked Berkeley right off the bat. They served pitchers of beer at LaVal's, like Scholz' in Austin where I had whiled away so many pleasant hours.

What we did was bold, impetuous, probably ill considered. We were in California, living in an efficiency apartment in Berkeley on California Street. Everything was different. In about one year since we met, we had literally come a long way.

Things did not go well. I could not find a job. With 3 years of law school but no degree, there was no place to go. I could not qualify to take the California bar exam. No one wanted to hire me as a non-lawyer, figuring I would soon become a lawyer and leave their company. Nancy had a degree in fine art but she could not find a job either. She was after all pregnant and any employer would have her taking maternity leave in only a few months. We were living on money I had borrowed from student loan funds and the money was running out.

Our forté had been laughing and playing, running away. This was the real world we were up against. Nancy became convinced that I would not pressure Helen to finalize the pending divorce and that I would not marry her. On a drunken evening, it all fell apart in an alcoholic quarrel. The booze was always there, getting us wrought up in good ways and bad, keeping us from calm, rational discussion. I felt she had gotten hysterical that night; she felt I was too indecisive to act to protect her and our baby. Voices were raised, threats made. She called her parents the next day and they wired money for one airline ticket to Texas. We parted at the airport.

I honestly believed I would never see her again and suddenly life lost all color, went gray, everything was in slow motion. Did I feel like daddy when mother left? I was alone in the bay area, suddenly hopeless, but I had the '55 Merc with good tires to get me back to Texas where it seemed I belonged. It was the second time I had gotten myself far away and longed for home, for Texas, specifically for the Hill Country and Austin. I set the all-time record driving back—only stopping for cheap sleep at a large YMCA in Tucson, and then only because I had begun to hallucinate from exhaustion and heartache.

After Nancy slipped away at the San Francisco airport in 1964, I went in for indiscriminate and frequent sexual liaisons. I remained married to Helen who was a saint, but I copulated at every opportunity. There were copious opportunities; it was the '60s. No one ever satisfied me. I searched the faces of all of these women for the qualities, the magic of Nancy. I still dreamed of her endlessly. It would be eight long years of separation before she miraculously returned to me in an old Volvo station wagon.

The last chance came on February 18, 1965, or thereabout, a few days after our son was born at Baylor Hospital in Dallas. She had agreed to meet me. I was out of school with the law degree but no job or good prospects of one when I went to Dallas the night before and was awake all night thinking, thinking. What could be done to keep the baby? There was no answer I could get hold of. I saw Nancy only a few minutes that day and it was all over. She did not propose to keep the baby as a single mother since she had tried and failed to do that with her child born of a teen-age marriage and divorce too young. Her son lived with her parents, and she desperately wanted to reclaim him. Our son was adopted soon thereafter and we have never had contact with him. I had just finished law school, for what that was worth.

Outside of Austin

It has been hard to extricate myself from the law though I've come a long way, working out from under the pile of files with Molly, my dependable quadralegal.

I have always had a love-hate relationship with the law. I come to believe I want out; but then, given the right circumstances, I want to speak for some poor soul accused or injured, to stand up for some principle like free speech. And I am far from ashamed of these impulses.

To say I hated law school is to vastly understate the truth of it. I truly despised every minute of it except courses in Constitutional Law, a Civil Rights seminar, International Law, and occasionally torts and criminal law. This was to mirror my interests in the actual practice of law. (Sadly, I never figured out how to get into international law.) Law school is the grind it has been portrayed as in literature and film. One needs to be compulsive-obsessive and have a very high tolerance for boredom.

Someday I hope someone somewhere figures out how to teach the law in a way that is alive, intellectually stimulating and less didactic. I doubt they will. Law may just be inherently dull and pedantic. Had I known what it was actually like, I am sure I never would have chosen to go to law school. I put zero importance on mastery of the law itself or effectiveness in court for its own sake. It was how the law could be used to further other objectives that provided the spark for me. It was only a means to an end.

At graduation from UT law school I had gotten a grant from Law Students Civil Rights Research Council (called "Lis-creeg"), an adjunct of the National Lawyers Guild, to go into the South for civil rights work. I was assigned to the Southern Regional Office of the ACLU in Atlanta directed by the colorful Chuck Morgan, a hell of a trial lawyer who had been run out of Alabama for his liberal views on civil rights.

The main work was suits in the states of the South for voting rights. I was housed, rent-free, in a Mennonite house, which given my lifestyle, was a strain on all. I did not last as long as I could have received the monthly stipend of $50, but it was an honor to be in close contact with the historical legal work happening there.

Outside of the free unconventional first year Helen and I were together, the best year for us would turn out to be the year and two months we lived, miserably it seemed at the time, in Houston after Nancy and law school were both seemingly done.

Upon returning to Austin after Nancy and I had run off to San Francisco, the reality of finishing the truncated voyage law school had been for me set in. The last semester in the fall of 1964 was an agony of debt piling up, guilt accumulated, losses borne.

I took the bar exam in October while still in law school, and immediately afterward, I came down with viral pneumonia. Right after that, I was "tried" for an honor code violation at school. I felt like Job. Acquitted, back to health, duly licensed to practice law in the great State of Texas, law degree bestowed, I found I had to leave Austin if I was to be employed. We were living amidst bounced checks and privation.

In spring of 1965, I got a job in Houston. It was meager pay for a lawyer but any pay was welcome after several months of looking and years of living at subsistence level. Tom Lay, a solo practitioner in Pasadena, hired me as an associate, and a new chapter opened up for me. He had what in those days was called a general practice; the creeping age of specialization was still a decade from overtaking us.

I had been sleeping on the vinyl couch of a friend in Houston. My much-traveled 1955 Mercury (the car that had taken Nancy and me to San Francisco and I had driven back alone), was ailing badly. After I started as a lawyer in Pasadena, I got up each morning and had to put oil and transmission fluid in the Merc. I did this dressed in one of my two suits each day before cranking it up and hitting the Gulf Freeway.

Helen and Pooh (my daughter was called Pooh by everybody until she was in junior high) still lived in Austin; I had to work a month or two, get paid, and then I could move them to Houston. I had one light colored cotton suit, which I bought at Monkey Ward's for $19.95, and an olive colored cotton suit I had bought at Goodwill for $5.00. I alternated wearing these two suits throughout that first summer of 1965 in the tropical clime of Houston as I took my first tentative steps as a lawyer.

Actually, I was fearless in the way one is when he doesn't know enough to be scared. I ventured with little hesitation into places angels feared to tread. But I never got bushwhacked and so I had learned this: boldness is a good trait for a lawyer. Later I would learn the opposite.

Life had taken me from Waco in the early years to Dallas and finally to the Valhalla, Austin. Now I was removed against my fervent desire and transplanted to Houston, a city I had never wanted to live in, home of Lamar High School, our archrival in debate. The LA of Texas: too big, too full of yahoos, too industrial.

But Houston had recently gotten a major league baseball team, a fact that registered solidly in the good range. I never got over my boyhood passion for baseball. From my first dazzling view of the minor league Katy Park in Waco in the '40s, I was hooked on baseball.

I had been a Cleveland Indians fan in the `40s and `50s. In 1965 the Houston Astros stepped up to the plate in the country's first domed stadium which opened almost to the day of when I went to my first law office in the Houston suburb.

All that had happened with Nancy–falling in love, running off, defeat, losing our son and then each other–lay in a murky past but still stung. I had a broken heart in the old Irish tradition and in the same tradition I was entitled to drown my sorrows.

But I had not lost my beautiful little blond girl child, Pooh. I spent a lot of time with her, taking her to the zoo at Herman Park. Even our after work watering hole, an icehouse on Alabama Street, was selected for being a place where you could take a small child. Sometimes I could not bring myself to leave her at day care and we would find some amusement strolling the University of Houston campus, my sanctuary in the big, cold-hearted city.

The terms of life had changed drastically after eight years at universities as a student. I now faced "real life," earning a living, repaying the considerable debt I had accumulated while going to school, thinking of my daughter's future needs. So I promptly developed a duodenal ulcer at the ripe age of 26.

I had been accustomed to lots of time to myself in Austin. In Houston, I suddenly had no time to myself. I fought to carve out an hour and a half for lunch which I spent at the UH library reading. Once I took a day off and spent the whole day in bars near the campus, ruminating about my life and what was happening to it, the loss of any interior life.

As she was throughout our years together, Helen was a stalwart of support. She knew I was suffering, but I suspect she knew it would pass, too. I tended to take myself far too seriously! Helen had been a proofreader at the University of Texas Press and she got jobs in Houston, first at Gulf Publishing, then at the University of Houston Press. Together we were making much more money than we were accustomed to having.

In Austin, I had spent a lot of time at the library of the Episcopal Seminary over near Eastwoods Park. I discovered it in the spring of 1961 when I lived a block away. It was very quiet and uncrowded. I did what little writing I ever did at the library there in 1961 to 1965. The law caught up with me and took over with the move to Houston.

A doctor had prescribed the obscure tranquilizer Compazine for my ulcer–the anxiety I had and the difficulty eating. After two or three months taking this drug daily, a strange thing happened. One morning in July I woke up and I had no drive, no ability to move at all. There was in my mind a cavernous emptiness, all initiative was gone and I could not summon any.

I called in sick, or Helen called in for me. All three of us went to Galveston where I lay on the beach all day trying to figure out what was happening to me. Eventually I figured out that it was the Compazine that robbed me of all initiative, and also it was an early (and mercifully short) encounter with depression.

This interloper was to reappear many times and take me to the bottom of my life, before I got treatment and overcame it in the first year of my sobriety. The treatment was a drug, nortriptyline, a tricylic antidepressant, which I still have to take everyday to control the potentially fatal disease of depression. I am certain that I am alive because of this treatment, this drug.

I know that depression and alcoholism killed my father. Neither disease was effectively controlled before they got him. Thankfully, for me they have been.

In a sense, I was depressed for most of the fourteen months we lived in Houston and Pasadena. The one shining light of this period was my little girl. Pooh was only two years old when we moved to the area. She was talking a little. Once in her crib she looked at me and asked when we were going home. I felt the same way. When were we going home to Austin?

Across from Herman Park, out front of the Warwick Hotel there is a traffic circle of sorts. In the middle of it is a large fountain where water flows up and tumbles down. Each time we would pass it, Pooh would say "Wadu." I probably drove around that fountain a lot more than was necessary to hear my daughter say wadu. Curiously, it brightened my day.

Our first apartment was on Telephone Road, a disaster. Finally, I figured out that aside from the blinking neon sign outside our bedroom window, it was the utter lack of any grass or growing things that made it so depressing.

Soon we found a small but pleasant apartment on West Clay in the Montrose area with a convenience store right across the street. We were drinking beer every night but, by later standards, a fairly small amount. Directly across from our place was a large duplex. There we discovered a sweet old (old to us) lady who already kept two other little girls about 2 on the weekdays. Everyone called her Mama Mooney.

Finally, there was a day care arrangement for my angel that I could feel good about. Pooh loved Mama Mooney, as did Laurie and Robin, the other two precious little girls. This one breakthrough, as well as a fairly pleasant place to live, improved my life greatly.

It was dawning on me that things could fall into place and life could be better if you tried. By fall of 1965, my angst was under control. A sort of truce with Houston obtained. Life was more than just bearable.

After work I hung out with the lawyers at Dixie & Schulman, my longtime friend from high school days, George Dixie, only a year ahead of me, Bob Hall and Harry Jones, two of the most amiable, interesting and liberal lawyers I have ever known. We drank beer at a greasy spoon grill called Little Paul's a block from the courthouse. All under the senior supervision of Chris Dixie, a tenured labor lawyer and political operator in Harris County who had great influence in the Democratic Party.

These times often went on into the humid late evenings as George, Bob, Harry and I found other watering holes, even, I hate to admit now, strip joints. Talk of politics and law inspired me to hope and believe that there were great possibilities ahead.

At that time I still believed in the model of the liberal lawyer, fighting for civil rights and the poor and unpopular, but personally well off and respectable, somewhat removed from the streets and jails where the battle was joined. Certainly my drinking buddies at Little Paul's were approaching this in their practice. Several generations of lawyers had been deeply influenced by the life and legal work of Clarence Darrow.

But my first job as an associate in a law office ended abruptly when my employer took ill and after a few weeks could no longer afford my able assistance. Perils of the solo practitioner. Without missing a payday, I was hired as the first Assistant City Attorney of Pasadena in the brand new law department of the city. City Attorney Jim Riggs was the first full-time employee of the city; past city attorneys had been private practitioners who provided contract legal service to the municipality.

I soon discovered that the city's legal affairs were hopelessly botched up. My boss was a night owl who worked into the wee hours but overslept until noon. I had no fear of being late to work in the mornings heading out the Gulf Freeway. Riggs would rarely show up before 2 p.m. That suited me. I was never a morning person.

As soon as my boss showed up the whole suite of offices for the Law Department filled with the soft jazzy sounds of Herb Alpert and the Tijuana (pronounced incorrectly as "Tia-juana") Brass. The job paid better than my stint in the private law office, although the opportunity for learning and real legal experience was much greater in my former little law office above the Southmore Savings and Loan Association.

The time came when I could no longer tolerate the incredibly petty municipal politics that spilled into the Law Department. Also, city employment required one to actually reside within the city limits of Pasadena. We deplored living there. The air was polluted by nearby industry. The town was a nightmare of monolithic culture, all white Protestants whose only virtue was that they were by and large working people. Unionism was strong, as it had been with the painters I grew up with, my dad's milieu. It was definitely not enough to redeem Pasadena.

In late spring of 1966, my situation erupted and I departed the City of Pasadena Law Department. Living in the Montrose area, getting out of Pasadena for 16 hours of every workday and the whole weekend, had made it tolerable to work there. The Montrose area of Houston was already starting to take on an interesting diversity, sophisticated funkiness and counter-culture feeling. And it was on the verge of trendiness. Alas, Pasadena had virtually nothing that redeemed it.

In July I traveled to Austin again (I had gone back looking for a job) and had the plain old Irish luck to call my friend Ronnie Dugger, editor of the Texas Observer, at the right time. Representatives of the Office of Economic Opportunity (OEO), the federal war on poverty agency, were in Austin looking to hire a lawyer or journalist to be the Office of Inspection man in the Southwest Regional Office in Austin. Dugger referred me to Peter Spruance, the OEO guy from Washington, D.C., who interviewed me.

He concluded by saying the job had three big drawbacks: you would have to live in Austin, do a lot of traveling and do a lot of writing. These seemed like outstanding perks to me. I was ecstatic to be hired in this new national campaign against poverty. And the money was grand compared to my last two jobs. Back then people would wink and speak of "getting paid in the five figures" because any salary of $10,000 a year or higher was very good pay indeed.

It was a triumphant return to Austin that summer of 1966. A town that I had been unable to get a job in to save my life after law school.

I loved the OEO job, traveling in the five state region and frequently to Washington, writing of the inspection trips I made, learning from some tough old journalists how to write sparingly and to the point. We were the "eyes and ears of Sargent Shriver" under the leadership of Pulitzer Prize winning journalist, Edgar May. There was a tremendous opportunity to aid the good guys, the poor who were organized and mobilized in the Community Action Programs seeking change. And to meet the movers and shakers, activists who were in the War on Poverty at one level or another.

I stayed so busy until it fell apart for me in late 1967 that I forgot to stay in the bag. I even forgot to philander. I remained true to my wife for a record number of months and sober too, much of the time. The work with community action programs in the five-state area kept me virtuous. I was putting in some 15- and 16-hour days on the road and long hours of writing when I came home.

We had rented a brick two-bedroom house in Austin on the outskirts of the neighborhood I would later embrace and reside in for over three decades, Clarksville. Life had settled in a bit and I found meaning in the work and I was seeing Pooh grow up.

The memory of Nancy and the deep feelings I had for her would not be banished. Every woman I saw or made love to was seen in relation to Nancy and no one could measure up. After her no one else would do though if I could have made it work with Helen I would have because she was such a good person. But the way it was in the early '70s neither of us was happy.

From spring of 1965–actually from the bleak, painful February morning around the time Nancy gave birth to our son and he was given up for adoption– until the last of 1967 I was monogamous. The pattern was that I became restless and dissatisfied and things happened.

It had all started on a peculiarly depressing December afternoon in New Orleans late in 1967. I had been a soldier in the War on Poverty working for the federal agency OEO (Office of Economic Opportunity) for a year and a half. In one of the domestic programs he pushed through Congress which LBJ could take pride in, the War on Poverty was the latest greatest hope for bringing real life in America into line with the picture we were all fed in school. Inspired by Michael Harrington's book "The Other America", about poverty in our nation, it was part of Kennedy's vision for the New Frontier.

I came on board in summer 1966 when it seemed we could actually empower the poor and raise them up out of hopelessness and destitution. Not since the early days of the New Deal had such idealism flourished in a federal agency. It was something I threw myself into. Traveling throughout a five state Southwestern Region of OEO, there were good times, as when a large group of Head Start kids sang to me in deepest rural Arkansas. There were scary times, as when I spoke in a black church in rural Louisiana with too many big windows amid warnings of nightriders with guns on the loose.

The bad times were the instances when we were thwarted from accomplishing the mission. On assignment in New Orleans one day in late 1967, the cumulative defeats, the realization that establishments everywhere were going to prevail in contests with OEO-spawned people's groups or community action organizations, hit me and staggered my zeal to go on with OEO. I had been too controversial myself for Washington and, hence there in New Orleans I was forbidden to have contact with community action groups or especially, black militants. My own emerging political radicalism was known to the higher ups.

I had inspired critical editorials, complaints from mayors in places where the community action poverty programs succeeded in rocking the boat. There was even a congressional hearing on complaints about OEO, where my name came up in connection with a shooting incident between students and police at predominately black Texas Southern University in Houston. My only part in it was to investigate for OEO. Apparently, in my report to OEO I had sided too much with the black students pinned down in their dorms by police gunfire. I sat 30 feet from the witness, an aide to the mayor of Houston, as I was vilified. It amused me but I was not amused by the way what happened at TSU that day was twisted and distorted by public officials or the way they sought to lay blame for rebellious ("uppity?") blacks on the War on Poverty.

But the federal OEO administrators wanted social change without upsetting the local power elites. You can't make an omelet without breaking any eggshells. Many of those with power thought I was too biased in favor of those who lacked it and they were right. So in my final field trip for OEO I was seeing a lot of Head Start sites, groups of 5 year olds, which hardly consumed my time.

One day in New Orleans I was lying in my hotel bed, drinking scotch, watching the movie "Bonzo Goes to College" on TV and I realized the War on Poverty was over for me. I could no longer believe in what we were doing. The real excitement I felt when I signed on was extinguished by what I had seen happen time and time again as community groups, believing the OEO rhetoric, got organized and eventually came in conflict with their local establishment. The agency subverted them, sold them out, one way or another, as political pressure built up to the boiling point.

It was happening in New Orleans that day even as I watched Bonzo (without Ronald Reagan this time) go to college. I could not even consort with the good guys. It was to be another lost battle for the poor.

I got up and wandered out to the campus where I had participated in so many school debate tournaments at Tulane University. Sitting there depressed, partially drunk–the logy downside of drunk–I came to a decision to quit the high paying job with OEO, hang out the proverbial shingle and try to be a good lawyer, in the second sense of the term. I wanted to be a one man ACLU; it was a fine dream, not a practicable one. The concept was hazy; the prospects dim, going on nothing but inspiration, so of course it worked.

Songs of Revolution

I am transported by the music of Phil Ochs perhaps more than any other. Molly's taste runs to Olivia Newton John and Abba.

When I graduated in January 1965, I had no prospects for a job. My grades were mediocre at best, ranging from 89 in Constitutional Law from famed law professor Charles Alan Wright to 60 in Property Law. The only course I actually failed in law school was Corporations. I was rather proud of failing that.

It is surely presumptuous as hell, but I thought of myself as having the same relationship to the law as Woody Guthrie did to music. I did not aspire to be a good legal eagle so much as to fight the good fight. I did not shoot for commercial success. Indeed, I was so indifferent to money that I would be surprised at a vantage point some 30 years later, after I started to look back and see that I had made a living, kind of.

I had never worried about money, one way or another, and—surprisingly–I had never had to. There was no merit in being a good lawyer, meaning a technically proficient one. There was merit in being a good lawyer, meaning a lawyer who did good. I measured my success by the extent I could lawyer and have it serve to promote social change, individual rights, peace and, yes, love. I thought the law, or lawyering, could do this and I believe it did for much of the three decades plus I did it in earnest. In earnest for me. I could not do too much in earnest. Earnest was not my bag, to use a term of the hippie generation.

That is the way I saw the law: not an end in itself, not something majestic and exalted as an institution, but a vehicle for furthering values and beliefs. A way of being part of the larger struggle that our rhetoric of the time often romantically referred to as the Revolution.

After Labor Day in 1967, at a farmworkers' organizing rally, I met a woman nearly 10 years younger than I and truly beautiful. In the turbulent last few months of 1967, as I grew increasingly disenchanted with OEO and became more radicalized politically in the company of organizer Martin Wiginton, I had a short but enchanting romance with Lisa. OEO and American liberalism were turning me off but Lisa and the emerging New Left Movement were turning me on.

She knew I was married (they all did), but in the free love and nickel cannabis days of the Movement such impediments were easily disregarded. Moreover, marriage was a hopelessly bourgeois institution associated with that worst of all possible states: uptightness. I basically subscribed to this (convenient) view.

Lisa reminded me of Leslie, but she was more beautiful and far more delicate. Martin and I were trying to relate to the farmworkers movement. I had immense respect for Cesar Chavez and he remained one of my heroes. (I was fortunate enough to meet him in the '80s.)

Lisa was a college student at UT-Austin and farmworkers volunteer in the Rio Grande Valley of Texas. She was fairly tall, dark complexioned with jet black hair, that haunting look in her brown eyes that was at once innocent and vulnerable (like she knew enough of life to be wary but still interested; at least that's how I remember her). I was attracted to her instantly. The eyes always tell a lot about someone.

Somehow I managed to get her alone in the area of a meeting we were at in Houston and find out how to find her in Austin. Back there a few days later I did call her and we went for a drink at the old hallowed Iron Gate Club. It was before the era of mixed drinks across the bar in Texas but at the Iron Gate anyone could join the "private club" on the spot.

We huddled in candle light with our cocktails and aided by drink I found the words to tell her I was enormously attracted to her and wanted very much to make love to her. It was direct, granted, but it was the '60s and to my great surprise and delight, she accepted. We checked into a room at the Mount Vernon Motel in the Delwood Shopping Center on Interstate 35—it was the same motel Nancy and I had lit up about three years earlier.

Lisa wanted me to use a rubber, which I have never in my life carried. I've never been that optimistic, or prepared for a romantic encounter. I literally ran about 75 yards and back to a Gulf service station that thankfully had a condom machine in the men's room. I had seen these machines for years, getting slightly titillated at the thought of guys who bought them to use immediately in coitus. Now it was I who stood before a machine buying one of the things to facilitate a coupling I had a tremendous itch for.

When I got back breathlessly to the room, Lisa waited nude in the bed. We made love sublimely; even with the unaccustomed latex sheath, the chemistry was good. I was 28, she was almost 20. The world opened up to us in the rush of pleasure we gave each other. There is no feeling like it; no drug can take one to a better place.

We saw each other many times thereafter, making love mostly in borrowed apartments. She never asked me to use a rubber again. All I remember is tender and slow sex, after which Lisa once said with a deep sigh "You are such a good lover." That ratcheted my ecstasy up many levels and I've never forgotten it. The ego is after all an important sex organ.

She was a quiet, sensitive young woman, never given to saying such things to produce an effect. (There was another woman I met about a year later who had the practice of saying "It's so big" during sex and I knew it was just for effect.)

Lisa was first blossoming into her full womanhood and this thing we had found together seemed special. Maybe the more so because we had to do it furtively and maybe because we had so boldly grasped for it that day at the Iron Gate. This lovely, dark-eyed woman with that haunted look (in these respects so similar to Nancy) was the first one I had been with since I lost Nancy. I had made no serious effort or come upon any real opportunity though I wanted someone. I thought of the Iron Gate romancing as a seduction–and maybe it was, but I wonder now who was seducing whom.

Moreover, I have discovered a well kept secret, at least for my generation: the girls and women wanted to do it as much as I did. Even though I sometimes felt I had led them to it, I know now they were very willing and even desirous of lovemaking. I was never any Lothario, but intercourse, even sexual play and fondling which early on had resulted in orgasm, often seemed like a victory of some kind. It was the glorious '60s, the Age of Aquarius with its freedom from norms, taboos and inhibitions, which allowed me to see that both sexes really wanted the same thing.

I don't think that any decade of the 20th century was more fun to be young in than the '60s. No AIDS, no fear, no sweat. The old prudish sexual morality was out the window. Drugs, including alcohol, were in. My own drug of choice was always alcohol. I used marihuana a lot, cocaine many times, speed a few times and acid once. Mostly I preferred being whacked on booze. And I stayed that way.

However, the aspect of my bohemian hedonism that I regret is the pain I caused Helen who was entirely undeserving of it. When the flings were over or in remission, Helen was the person I would have long, soul-searching conversations with and she was the one who would help me get back to a safe place. To dry out, to come down, to get grounded again. I could always talk to her. We remained good friends for 20 years after we were divorced. During that time I had no better friend, although after we got sober together Nancy has been my best friend and our relationship has matured and broadened so that I have not wanted or needed to wander.

To my mind, anyway, Helen and Nancy surpassed all other women in my life by virtue of one attribute, intelligence. And with each of them I was following the advice that Maury Maverick gave me: find one good woman and let her protect you from all the rest. Trying and failing with Helen but that was not her fault.

In spring of 1968, a mass demonstration at UT gave me an influx of work and my first exposure to real leaders of the anti-war and civil rights movements. SDS leaders, particularly Greg Calvert, were to have a substantial influence on the concept and direction of my developing legal persona. Perhaps most important was my friend and comrade, the best political organizer I've ever known, Martin Wiginton. Greg helped me develop a theoretical notion of being a radical lawyer while Martin, knee deep in the big muddy, sent the clients my way in batches as he worked tirelessly in the trenches.

I drank away many long nights with Martin, even before I left OEO, as together we felt our way toward being part of the struggle we later spoke of as The Revolution. If we ran out of hooch at 2 a.m. after hours, we dug into the pantry for cooking sherry or anything with alcohol and continued the political talk.

Again, my memories of this period have a definite musical accompaniment. The songs of protest–Pete Seeger, Phil Ochs, Tom Paxton, Peter, Paul & Mary, Buffy St. Marie, Joan Baez, Eric Anderson, even old Bob Dylan. They sing those classic folk songs of the '60s rousingly in my memories of that rich and exciting political time, unparalleled in my lifetime. Sitting with Martin reveling in the music, an aura of alcohol hanging heavy in the air; it was reminiscent of listening to my dad's dreams on late weekend nights.

The difference is that something came of these '60s nights. We found ways to be relevant to the change trying to come about in our country. Martin was a defrocked lawyer; he had voluntarily renounced the profession. We both became increasingly driven to radicalism by the frustrations, disappointments and dead-ends of liberal politics. Especially the debacle of Texas electoral politics and the failed War on Poverty (Martin worked for OEO briefly while I was there). We were ready to march to the beat of a different drummer.

In late '67 we both declared ourselves liberated from liberalism. Martin became a full-time radical organizer. I hung that damn shingle out across the street from the Travis County courthouse. Like many others in America, we left the flaccid Democratic Party.

As if to underscore this break, we went in late 1967 to the National Conference for New Politics held at the Palmer House Hotel in Chicago, where over 5,000 multi-racial radicals convened to talk of a new politics. It was the only time I had seen and heard Martin Luther King, Jr. in person. He had publicly come out against the war in Viet Nam.

The greatest intellectual stimulation was the on-going dialogue with Greg Calvert, who became my friend. Through him and others, I learned of and from the writings of people like Herbert Marcuse (New Left theory) and the lives of people of conscience like David Dellinger, whose very lives are the opus of their beliefs. (There are actually few people like Dave; he is one of a kind, a moral and political giant whose life instructs us by example. I was fortunate enough to meet and speak with David in 2003, a few months before he died.)

Greg Calvert was a transplant to Texas having been in the Midwest and Pacific Northwest for most of his 31 years. He had been a college instructor, a national SDS officer, a sexual adventurer in the gay scene of Paris. When I met him he was married to Carol Nieman, also an intellectual, a brilliant and good person. Heterosexuality, or bi-sexuality, failed Greg in the '70s and he lived as an openly gay man, with his partner Ken Carpenter for 29 years. I am proud he was my friend until he died in 2005, even though he left Texas in 1981.

Greg caused me to think critically, not simply react to acculturation, about homosexuality and bi-sexuality. Other than Greg and his partner Ken, I have known almost no gay men (who were "out"). But because I got to know and learn from Greg and other gay and lesbian folks, I supported gay liberation.

Our firm was involved in cases involving gay people and groups, notably a protracted bit of litigation on behalf of a gay group at Texas A&M seeking approval as a campus organization and calling itself Faggies. One of my last cases involved a gay Army officer who was kicked out of the Army for telling in violation of the ludicrous "don't-ask-don't-tell" policy concerning homosexuality in the military. During all the years of practice I handled military cases that I probably would never have gotten into except for the war in Viet Nam.

When I went on my own in Austin on January 1, 1968, I expected to last a year or two. Or maybe I simply had no particular expectations. It was easier then to truly live in the moment.

It was a smashing time to have a law license, perhaps the best time in the history of this country. Revolution was afoot; the Warren Court still reigned supreme on the law. Things were being done in the courts that were never done before, or since. The accessibility that the poor, black, Hispanic, young and simply bold had to our courts was unprecedented.

I had to do a lot of ordinary legal work (lucky to get any in Austin in 1968) to pay for the good I could do. But I was busy from the start. There was no one else in Austin or, as far as I knew, the Southwest, trying to do what I was doing. There was the venerable labor lawyer, my friend, Sam Houston Clinton, Jr., a lawyer I respected immensely. He did a lot of the ACLU work and he got little reward for his considerable pro bono efforts. When I plunged into depths over my head, almost daily, I called upon Sam and he readily helped me.

Sam was my mentor in the daily fire fights of the law; even as my guru of good lawyering was the legendary Maury Maverick, Jr. in San Antonio. Maury and I were to become immersed in the business of representing conscientious objectors to the war in Viet Nam. Both Sam and Maury were vintage examples of the best of senior practitioners of that era, the very best. Maury would become like a surrogate father to me.

Upon opening the door to my modest office, I already had two clients. Enrique Madrid was a very idealistic University of Texas student whose conscientious objection to war was sneered at by his local draft board and he got an order to report for induction into the Army, which he refused. He was indicted by a federal grand jury. I can't remember how he got to me but he retained me as his lawyer.

A month or two into my private practice in Austin I stood inwardly quaking with my client before federal Judge Adrian Spears in San Antonio, Texas. Before that day I had prepared a Motion to Dismiss and brief in support that was about 100 pages long, albeit the font of type was different in all three sections of the brief and the Motion, having been typed by four volunteers working at the deadline on four very different typewriters (a machine widely used in the last century). I had gathered material for a Nuremburg defense from Maury Maverick as well as the CO status Enrique had been denied. My research had yielded a point of law involving due process at the draft board that won the case. Maury came to court to give me moral support.

Fully prepared to go to prison for his convictions, Enrique left the courtroom free of all criminal charges. By covenant with myself, I waited 'til I got to the outskirts of town to let out a coyote yell, the first of many.

My other case was a divorce for Chuck Cairns, a history or government professor at UT. Hiring me to represent him had been a political act, as many of his actions were. Indeed, as my reputation spread on campus and in progressive circles, many clients with ordinary legal matters came to me as a way of supporting the Movement, whether they would have put it that way or not. (One of these was Tom Moriarty, who has been my good friend ever since.)

I had left the high paying Government job and simply started in private practice in Austin hoping to represent the activists of the New Left that flourished in Austin in the late '60s. Also, I was drawn to the law after two years away (working for OEO). The taste of practice I got in Houston had whetted my appetite for more.

I believed good could be done and I relished the job of advocating for people seeking justice. I can't deny this conventional aspect of my launching into practice on my own. After four decades, I still feel a thrill in undertaking and accomplishing something for a client. There is that pay-off one feels from doing something to help another. It is a part of law practice and I hope it always will be.

Huge law cartels and narrow specialization are threatening to end it. Professionalism and the "bottom line" rule. It does not bode well for the future. In 1968, I had rented a basement office in a building across the street from the Travis County Courthouse. I invested in a swivel chair and an Ireland poster for the wall and two plastic client chairs. (Fortunately someone had abandoned a desk in the office I rented.) I took calls on the landlord-lawyer's line. Overhead: about $150 per month.

I had already taken the case of Enrique Madrid, a draft resister who had refused induction and been indicted in federal court. Also, I had agreed to represent a UT professor and friend, reputedly a Trotskyite, in his divorce proceeding. There was a caseload for you.

Still feeling the disappointment of what I perceived as the failure of the War on Poverty, to which I had given much of myself, and the default of Texas liberals who dodged the issue of the war in Viet Nam, I wrote an article for the Texas Observer entitled "Liberation from Liberalism". It was my manifesto of radical coming out.

Over the next few months I got cases of many kinds, but things took off in the spring when a bunch of students set up a large demonstration on the Drag outside the gas station of Don Weedon, who had been loudly racist and was accused of attacking black students. Everyone was arrested and charged mostly with unlawful assembly, a few with more and some with less serious counts. It was the opportunity for someone like myself to step up and I did. So did Bobby Caldwell, a black attorney from Houston.

We got into a protracted legal battle that took us into federal court to enjoin the prosecutions, which we did for over a year, defending half a dozen jury trials, one with six defendants, half of them defending themselves intent on making it a forum for their political views, with which none of us had any problem.

The defendants were the people singled out as ring leaders by the infamous Bert Gerding, the head of the "red squad" at the Austin Police Department; my client, SDS'er Sue Jankowski; Larry Jackson, the SNCC organizer represented by Bobby Caldwell; Dick Reavis, the bantam guru of the Progressive Labor faction of SDS at the University; Bob White; and a third member of PL, Chester Wilson, all of them representing themselves.

It was wild and woolly. Dick Reavis at one point told the jury, in effect, after the revolution anyone who says racist things is immediately whisked off to jail. I practically fell off my chair. We had been talking to this jury all during the trial about how important the First Amendment guarantee of Free Speech was. (I should say that in adult life, Reavis has distinguished himself as a writer.)

I cannot recall the verdict. I think some or all were convicted. I do remember that no one did any jail time. For all the work I did on these cases, there was no fee, but it did cement a relationship for me with the activists in SDS and SNCC.

The very last "Weedon" case involved Enrique Madrid, the client in the first draft case which I had won in federal court a year earlier. He could have pled for a small fine but he was always a man of principle and demanded a full jury trial.

Through the process of defending these cases over a year and a half, the pundits at Scholz' Bier Garten had been critiquing our efforts, especially the liberal lawyers with quaint notions of trial work. For this shindig I recruited two of them, Sam Houston Clinton, the very experienced labor and ACLU lawyer, and the colorful Brooks Holman, who was destined to die very young. The three of us strode into the courtroom of Judge David McAngus with Enrique. Talk about overkill.

All of us had different levels of experience and notions of strategy and we ran the jury ragged, first one then another of us popping up in court. Brooks got a jury panel member so mad in the voir dire I thought the venire man was coming out of the box to clock him. Sam was the wise and aloof scholar of appeal points he carefully preserved and monitored, going back to his office to type up bills of exception on his little portable typewriter.

All was apparently lost when the judge, who had made up his mind the client was out there that day so he must be guilty, overruled our good-as-gold motion for a directed verdict on the grounds that the state wholly failed to offer any evidence on one element of the offense. The prosecutors had much egg on their faces but the judge saved them public embarrassment. The verdict of guilty was publicized and on our unpublicized motion for new trial a month later the case was dismissed by the chastened prosecutors who knew full well they had screwed up.

I can remember a conversation one day in my office with one of the SDS leaders, Greg Calvert, in which I declared that I would take action that most lawyers would not because I did not mind being branded as a radical lawyer; it was just what I was. And in that moment I realized what I had been trying to do, to become. There were a few other events that solidified my incarnation as a radical lawyer.

In 1968, I had gotten wind of a few lawyers meeting at the legendary Highlander Folk School near Knoxville, Tennessee, to talk about mobilizing lawyers to represent the growing numbers of Movement people needing legal help, one way or another. The local Movement people passed the hat to pay my way out there.

It was the first time that I met Bill Kunstler, Arthur Kinoy and Ben Smith. Also present was Ann Braden, an incredible organizer with the Southern Conference Educational Fund or SCEF. (My memory is uncertain as to whether Kinoy was there. But none of the participants I remember are still alive, including Arthur.) These terrific folks indulged the novice and listened with genuine interest to the plight of activists in Austin and Texas.

Two important events came more or less from that meeting. First, the infamous Wimberley Conference at a dude ranch in, naturally, Wimberley, Texas, took up a weekend and left a mess. There were a couple hundred Movement people and a few dozen lawyers who were being pressed to do more to provide legal assistance to the Movement.

I was on the program as one of the panelists in a discussion that included Bernardine Dohrn, later a leader in the SDS Weatherman faction. Kunstler was the keynote speaker, but Charles Garry, who defended the Black Panthers in California, also spoke. Almost every lawyer in Texas who had ever so much as taken an ACLU case showed up.

I've tried for years to figure out how to give the credit to Martin Wiginton and Greg Calvert for organizing this unique event without also giving them the blame. A great deal of alcohol was consumed and that led to some bizarre speeches from an open mike, mostly by the lawyers. However, bringing Movement people together with the lawyers who might be induced to help was beneficial, as later events showed.

The leader of the lawyers quickly proved to be Warren Burnett, who was renowned for his love of "ethanol", as he called booze. He was able to function at a very high degree, even with a load on.

My friend Dave Richards avers that he himself was sober, and in Dave's case, I believe it. He also took a leading role, as did Sam Houston Clinton (these two later became law partners in Austin until Sam was elected to the highest criminal appeals court in Texas).

I believe the legendary Maury Maverick was in attendance; if not, he was there in spirit. It is not surprising that these four Texas lawyers contributed more than any others of their generation of liberal lawyers to the defense of radical activists in their frequent scrapes with the authorities.

There were others who joined on various skirmishes such as Don Gladden, Chris Dixie, Bob Hall. Of my generation, Doran Williams, David Hall and lots of legal services lawyers gave free legal help. Also, resulting from the Wimberley Conference, Cam Cunningham decided to return to Texas from his legal services job in Arizona.

After working for OEO, and becoming disillusioned and radicalized, and in the face of the escalating war in Viet Nam and the on-going civil rights struggle, I craved relevance and I had found it. In the coming months I would get all the relevance I could handle and then some. I had become a member of SDS and the National Lawyers Guild–my colors were flying freely for all to see.

When I hung out the shingle January 1, 1968, and embarked on this odyssey, I got caught up in a series of sexual liaisons with many women for almost five years. It's a cliché, but they all run together. I look back on that time now and I see how much it had to do with ego and seeking pleasure as an antidote to anxiety. And I shudder to think of some of the women involved. But not all; most are still friends. Two died tragically young, likely victims of drug overdose.

To some extent, the women were perks to the role I took (or created) of Movement lawyer. Remember the cartoon that appeared in many underground papers: the depiction of a young woman saying, "women say yes to men who say no?" It was about draft resisters, but I swear it applied to lawyers who dared set up outside the main tent where lawyers had been kept, and who shared the risks and excitement of struggle for radical social change.

Living our convictions in a holistic new way was a model taking shape at that exciting time. We were Movement people first and lawyers second. Our aim was not just to be technically proficient in the profession but to use our law degrees to stand with our brothers and sisters in a larger struggle for the country, our country.

Perhaps our idealism outstripped our judgment, particularly with regard to how hard it would be to do. But the love and support of the Movement did carry us through and enable us to grow in a way as lawyers we could not have done before the advent of the New Left in America.

If we had to mop the barracks floor occasionally, we also heard "yes" a lot from women. We got cold beer, rosé wine and pot to smooth out the aftermath of battles in the streets or in the courts. The music of the '60s, I still believe, was the best ever in quality and abundance and it was the sound track of a Movement that valued song, dance, love and yes, revolution. Not in blood but in tolerance and peace, in change of our institutions to eliminate suffering and affirm life.

Bold Marauders

My quadralegal, Molly, knew that I had always been ambivalent about the law. The love-hate relationship. To me there is no majesty in the law in and of itself. Anymore than a violin is beautiful music before it is played. The law is only an instrument. From the sublime symphony of the Warren Court years, we have passed into the cacophony of discordance of the Rehnquist Court years. Now we face the chilling prospect of another reign of the right-wing judges.

My nagging doubts about the legal profession didn't start with the downfall over time of the courts a quarter of a century ago which has continued into the new century. The doubts were there in law school even as the Warren Court did relatively glorious things with the law.

My old college roommate came to see me one day in 1968, my first year in private practice for myself. The two of us skipped out of my basement office across the street from the Travis County Courthouse, thinking to escape to the lake, as I loved to do in those days before the lakes were so developed that it was no escape. My friend had gone to law school at night down in Houston after a hitch in the Army. He worked in Pasadena in my old job as Assistant City Attorney. My old boss Jim Riggs with his constant playing of Herb Alpert music was long gone. The atmospherics were different, the pay even better than in my time there.

We went out to my favorite place, the Bull Creek Lodge, a marvelous funky place, not too thickly peopled. It was spring, so we could sit outside.

I was overwhelmed, as I liked to get in those days, with cases: about a hundred draft clients trying to avoid getting killed in Viet Nam, or even going, and dozens of UT students arrested in a civil rights demonstration near campus, the infamous Don Weedon case. My responsibilities so far exceeded my fees and time it was laughable. After only a few months, I was weary of jousting with the system.

I looked wistfully on the waters of Bull Creek, mentally still seeing visions of the lovely Nancy frolicking with me there, as we did so often in earlier times. I told my old roomie how dissatisfied I was with the practice of law. Not being idealistic and only interested in the law as a way to make a living, he scoffed. Finally, he said, "What would you rather be? If you could be anything at all, what would you want to be?"

It was a fair question, deserving of my truthful answer, and I thought on it for a minute before I said, "A Bold Marauder." No doubt he had never heard Richard and Mimi Fariña's song. But at that moment and now, nearly 40 years later, my greatest desire was/is to be a Bold Marauder. Though I could not articulate what I mean by that, it is personal and subjective, not reducible to words. The actual lyrics of the song are chilling. The idea of being a Bold Marauder, and perhaps a 20th century hero slaying dragons, called to me at some deep and mystical level. The limitations of everyday work and life had come to feel as binding as fetters of chain.

Over the years from 1968 to 1978 there were dozens of Bold Marauders ranging in age from 2 to 52. Born first as a stoned and boozy softball team with only one annual no-holds-barred game always played on the Sunday prior to Memorial Day at Pease Park on Shoal Creek. The game had been conceived at Scholz' garden one afternoon soon after my conversation at the Bull Creek Lodge. My younger hippie friend and client, Jay McGee, had thrown down a gauntlet (or did I throw it down?) and we agreed to meet on the softball diamond.

His team, the Zapatistas, were younger, more hirsute, more hippie-ish, rumored to include outlaws like drug dealers. Whether or not it did, they had a more gonzo cast to their team. Each side provided a keg of beer (I believe the first one for our side was donated by the proprietor of Scholz' Bier Garten, a client of mine).

The only rule of the game for each of the next 10 years it was played was you're out if you knock over someone's cup of beer. The pitcher would always throw up a grapefruit at some point in the game to be smushed messily by the hitter. Sometimes a base runner would be tackled and held down until the ball was thrown in from the outfield so he/she could be tagged out.

There were always about 20 or 30 people playing on each team. Everybody got to play. In this bizarre manner we played a couple of hours 'til all were too impaired to keep playing except the kids who then played on awhile.

Each year both sides tried to think up zany antics to spring on the other. One year Jay McGee rode from center field into home plate on a real horse wearing his huge Zapata sombrero to start the game. In 1974, our team had bumper stickers printed well before game time and sported them around town on our cars to psyche out the Zapatistas. Each side had tee-shirts. The Bold Marauder tee-shirt was designed by Nancy before the game in 1973 and we would get a batch silk-screened by our teammate Terry DuBose every subsequent year. One year the shirt read "Bold Fucking Marauders." The last year, 1978, it read: "A Decade of Decadence."

There was a pathetic pennant that in theory went to the winners each year but in truth was stolen, taken out of the country and each year the subject of burning inquiry: who's got the pennant? For some reason, it was often rumored to be in Columbia or Peru. I got photos of it in strange places sometimes, often from a main man Zapatista, "Jimmy Lee" Edwards, still my good friend. Yet, eventually it miraculously showed up.

It was impossible to determine who "won" the game and every year both teams claimed victory. One year the Zapatistas conspired to kidnap me before the game but the plot was foiled by the drunken ineptitude of certain Zapatista operatives, not to mention the crack intelligence unit of the Bold Marauders. Briefly, in 1970 there had been a Bold Marauders team in Dallas. But the classic was the annual Bold Marauders versus Zapatistas game in Austin and the Dallas team was minor league.

Anything anyone could think up was incorporated into the outlandish doings surrounding the game. The turnout got larger each year, many spectators in for a good party, all our kids, whoever wanted came out. By some miracle, given Austin's climate, the game never was rained out. Austin is notorious for stormy, wet weather on Memorial Day weekend. In 1981 (after the last game had been played in 1978), 13 people died from flash flooding mostly on Shoal Creek caused by heavy downpours during Memorial Day weekend in and around Austin.

In my mind, the war in Viet Nam is the single event that most influenced and shaped my generation. It was the first of what has turned out to be many invasions or aggressive foreign interventions carried out by the bi-partisan War Party with the two wings, Republican and Democrat. The illegality and immorality of Viet Nam were compounded by the brutal and bloody way we killed innocent civilians including women and children. Something horrible called napalm was being dropped on the peasants. For my generation, it pricked our conscience as nothing ever had and we grew resolved to stop the war, whatever we had to do, and in this we were joined by a great many returning American soldiers.

My entry into law practice was catalyzed by the war. My first cases and the most numerous types were draft cases, fighting the draft that was conscripting and sending so many thousands of men barely younger than I to the marshes and jungles of Viet Nam. It was the ghastly immorality of bombing and napalming civilians that turned me against the federal government (for which I worked at the time). The assassinations of the Kennedys and Martin Luther King, Jr. signaled an end of innocence, the beginning of cynicism and a new American nihilism. But it had been the atrocious war that turned thousands of us against our government. Mass murder, genocide–whatever you called it, we could not accept complicity in something so appalling.

From 1968 to 1977, the year our commune or law firm broke up, a great deal of the work we did was related to anti-war efforts. We sought parade permits for peace marches and use of facilities for radical events. We defended rebellious service members in courts-martial and hearings and provided legal support to the Oleo Strut, a coffeehouse in Killeen, and the Fatigue Press both run by Movement organizers. We advised and represented military personnel seeking Conscientious Objector status and release from the service as well as AWOL soldiers.

After the victory in the Madrid case, I began to get a lot of draft resistance and in-service CO cases. Draft counseling groups on campus and at the Methodist Student Center started referring copious cases over to my office. I began a practice of going to the Oleo Strut coffee house just off the base at Fort Hood once a week to give legal advice to lined up GI's. I took on a lot of courts-martial. Apparently there was a little known revolt going on inside the military. Cases were many, fees were few but I learned a lot about the Army, military law, and even organizing.

A highly effective organizer, Josh Gould (and later, David Zeiger) had come to Killeen, the town where Fort Hood is located, and was doing a great job. So great that Josh was busted for possession of marihuana which the cops planted in his car during a search of dubious validity. He was ably and successfully defended by Davis Bragg, a local liberal attorney I grew to respect very much.

I realized that all over the country there are some, not many, lawyers like Davis–quiet, decent, altruistic and committed to the principles of law that make possible civilized democratic society. I think many of my brethren at the bar and others think of them as a lot like Atticus Finch in the exceptional novel "To Kill a Mockingbird"–many lawyers were influenced by this prototype so wonderfully created by Harper Lee in the book.

In 1969 Cam Cunningham and I decided to travel to Black Mountain, North Carolina for the initial organizing meeting of Southern Legal Action Movement (SLAM). I had been in practice as a Movement lawyer in Austin for a couple of years then, and admittedly I was suffering the effects of an uneven battle, to say the least, and isolation from other lawyers doing the kind of work I did. I was discouraged, spending much time out at the lake in introspective reflection, drinking, making love and listening to the static filled radio accounts of Astros games.

In the summer of 1969, I renounced my year and a half law practice to live on Lake Travis near Hudson Bend. I rented a lake house a hundred feet from the water to recover my sanity, to be a writer, to love life again. It was an airy house with a large side screened in porch where I often slept on the balmy summer nights. It was an idyllic setting. An inordinate part of my time was consumed by red wine drinking and listening to Houston Astros baseball games. And fornicating.

Cam had been in Arizona at the Navajo Legal Services Program, by virtue of a Reginald Heber Smith fellowship. Upon returning, he wanted to get together in a new kind of law practice, building on what I had done.

Late in 1969, Cam and I set out for Black Mountain, North Carolina to go to the organizing meeting of an organization that stemmed from the Knoxville meeting where I met Kunstler and the others. It was the Southern Legal Action Movement (SLAM).

We made the trip to North Carolina with Cam's wife Chris and his 4-month-old son Ian. We had to abandon my new Saab along the way because in the small town where it broke down no mechanics had ever seen a Saab. We got Martin Wiginton to drive the Cunninghams' Rambler to us and we continued on.

By the time of the SLAM meeting, over a year and a half into my debut as the town's radical lawyer, I was definitely suffering a little burnout. But Cam was raring to get some relevance for himself. In a conversation that went deep into a fifth of Tom Moore and the wee hours one night in Black Mountain, we agreed to become law partners.

Then, while at the conference, we encountered some people from the New York Law Commune–Ann Garfinkle, Fred Cohn, Gerald and Carol Lefcourt. (I'm not sure they were all at the conference and I forgot one name.) When we heard their concept and methods for creating a really different kind of law office, we knew we had our model. Whereupon we piled into Cam's sturdy but clanky Rambler, along with Brooklyn lawyer Loni Levy, and followed them back to New York, where we met with them and saw their operation (located in a loft as I recall).

Cam and I left New York City that fall around the time of the Woodstock festival upstate. We were ready to get after it in Austin.

Back in Austin we started up what Time magazine called the third known law commune in America. (I believe the other one was in Detroit. Others sprang up, such as the well-known Bar Sinister in Los Angeles, and in Houston, the Prairie Street Collective. The latter group of our friends in Houston consisted of Larry Sauer, Rick Prinz, John Sayer, Jeff Skarda, Robert Finlay, Paul Avila, Ed Mallett and Frances Cruz.)

The principles were simple, yet for lawyers, revolutionary. First, all decisions were made communally with every member of the commune including legal workers having an equal say. Second was the concept of voluntary income limitation. Every lawyer would draw only the money for subsistence living expenses, no matter the actual income of the office, and any surplus would be donated to other Movement groups or organizations. Subject to collective decision, Movement or political cases would be taken without regard to fees, i.e., free, usually. To pay the freight, ordinary cases would be handled at the going fee rate. (Some types of cases were not taken such as, in recognition of women's lib, defending rape cases).

It was only later that terms like pro bono and public interest achieved currency among lawyers somewhat like us. Our focus was more radical than those terms connote.

I, and the firms we had, did so much handling of what they now call pro bono publico cases that when the state bar started asking for reporting of how much lawyers had done each year, I told them I was caught up until the 22nd century. Not all our pro bono was meant to be that way. Many clients simply couldn't, and some just wouldn't, pay. For cases that were "political", for lack of a better word, we charged lowered or no fee. This was the work and these were the clients we loved.

The downside of our unorthodox practice was that we had to handle ordinary legal cases–DWI's and other criminal cases, including a few murder cases, divorces, workers' comp and plaintiff's personal injury, which I got a heavy dose of in the '90s, not by design. But sometimes the ordinary cases were anything but.

In 1971, the traveling troop called FTA (variously said to mean Fun Travel and Adventure or Free the Army or Fuck the Army) came to Fort Hood in Killeen just north of Austin. The show they did was fantastic. It included Jane Fonda, Donald Sutherland, Joe McDonald of Country Joe and the Fish and folksinger Len Chandler. To no one's surprise, the Killeen school board refused our petition for FTA to use a local school auditorium.

The five shows over a weekend were done at the underground GI coffeehouse, the Oleo Strut, in Killeen. Every show was packed full. I spent the weekend as lawyer-on-the-scene, along with Sally Millett, legal worker from our office. (We called our secretaries legal workers and they often came with us on these "street lawyer" gigs.)

This was another case when I distinctly recall how damn much fun it was then. It was especially fun I think when we got to be with our clients outside the courtroom, in the streets, sharing the struggle, celebrating life, chugging the elixir, puffing weed and making love.

That Easter weekend turned cold in Killeen and our friends and comrades at Fort Hood provided Sally and me with genuine Government Issue Army fatigue jackets. I still have mine–one of the true trophies of being a Movement lawyer. Sally and I hung around backstage all weekend with the luminaries.

I remember Joe McDonald best. His segment came early, after a warm-up number and maybe a skit to get Jane Fonda out on stage. Then Country Joe did his thing, including the anti-war anthem "One-Two-Three, What Are We Fighting For?" and his incredible energy suffused the place and galvanized one and all. When he came off stage, he literally collapsed and sprawled out on the floor, absolutely drained. But he had lit up the joint and set the stage for the rest.

At that moment, like all those cheering GI's, it was impossible not to believe we were going to stop the war in Viet Nam. At the conclusion of the weekend, we were all on a natural high and went en masse to a hastily organized reception the ACLU had set up.

Upon seeing Sally and me in our fatigue Army jackets, Ann Richards (who I had known for years in Dallas and in the Young Democrats) began to cackle and in her best voice said: "Oh my God, this is great! Jimmy was a draft dodger." She was always funny and fun loving until her death in 2006.

However, I didn't have to dodge the draft. My Oak Cliff draft board had no difficulty filling its quotas as hardly any young men there went to college or got other deferments. But I did burn my draft card in a bar in 1965.

The prosaic world of litigation was, in contrast, undramatic 90 percent of the time. It happened that the FTA weekend brought no legal problems and I did not have to swing into action. I could not help remembering, it was not so back in the earliest of my Fort Hood on-the-scene endeavors.

I cannot recall who the clients were, a political group with ties to UT–maybe Student Mobilization–who were holding a rock concert in a park in Killeen for Fort Hood GI's. It was July the 4th, 1968 and I was enlisted to go along to the scene, lest there be legal problems. When we arrived at the park, the electric plug-in box was closed and locked. The amplifiers, electric guitars, and mike could not be used. The whole point was to be heard.

In my rookie naiveté, I just looked in a phone directory, found a listing for the City Electrician and called him. He said he did not know what the problem could be but came right over and opened the door to the plug-in box. The concert ramped up and a rock band started playing.

Next to the staging area, a middle-aged man and his family were grilling food. The man ripped off his apron and came running. It turned out he was the Chief of Police in Killeen, Don Cannon, and he was mad. The plug-in box had been locked on purpose to ruin the concert (which had been advertised and was legal to hold in that park).

Chief Cannon was "undercover" out there that day. But the cops and city administration had neglected to bring the City Electrician into the loop.

My inexperience in not going to an authority like the city attorney, but instead calling the City Electrician, paid off. They still hassled us for quite awhile, but after discussions, their threats of arrest and our threats of lawsuits, the concert went on.

For this work, the group had paid my fee with two Volkswagen tires for my bug. Not long afterwards, I set off on a short vacation to Padre Island in that VW bug with my wife. Both of my fee tires blew out on the way and we wound up spending a night in the cramped VW on the side of the road in the desolate 55-mile stretch of highway through the King Ranch to South Padre Island. Talk about fun.

In another case during the war, I represented two Army enlisted men who were charged with starting a riot on the base at Fort Hood. One was black and one was white. The case was serious; it had been referred to a General Court Martial, the highest level where the most severe punishment could be given.

It seemed that the best evidence against them was what they had confided in a sympathetic chaplain in counseling sessions. Moreover, they had specifically gone to him as a chaplain, not as simply a friend. He had offered religious advice and reassurances very much in his role as chaplain. The Army was about the task of compelling this chaplain to divulge things he had been told in confidence and to testify against his counselees. The chaplain did not want to do it, but he was in the Army and could be ordered to by a superior officer or the court.

An Article 32 "investigation" was convened, a procedure under the Uniform Code of Military Justice (the latter two words an oxymoron). It is a bit like a pre-trial hearing without the safeguards that separate the functions of a judge and prosecutor or investigator. Our strategy was to make a large fuss about violating the confidential relationship with the chaplain and the incendiary racial overtones, or the guile of the Army in prosecuting two privates, one black, one white.

I think these were sufficiently worrisome at Fort Hood, where many young men were deployed to Viet Nam, that in the year 1971, the better part of valor was to drop the charges, which they did. I wanted combat pay because the hearing where victory came was on the first business day after returning from the Boulder NLG convention with all the attendant partying. The lesson here was: sometimes you win one you really don't expect to. It is manna from heaven.

We were not that lucky in the notable case of Richard Chase, a conscientious objector, unrecognized as such by the Army. Richard refused training to serve in civil disturbances in this country. There had been racial unrest and outbreaks of rebellion in Watts, Newark and other places, not to mention the brutal police riot that occurred at the 1968 Democratic Convention in Chicago. Army troops were brought in to quell these civil disturbances. It was a disturbing spectacle to think of U.S. military troops engaging in armed combat against blacks and young people who had legitimate grievances underlying their surge into the streets. One such disturbance broke out in Los Angeles following the assassination of Dr. Martin Luther King, Jr.

At Fort Hood, the Army was taking some of its personnel into a special training for this kind of urban warfare, allegedly to put down the so-called rioters, usually African Americans. Our client would not submit to this training because he did not believe soldiers should be used against citizens of this country and he was conscientiously opposed to participating in it. Chase was given a General Court Martial.

My new law partner at the time, Cam Cunningham, and I teamed up to represent Richard. It was Cam's first experience with military justice and he was very nearly barred from the proceedings on appearance grounds. Cam weighed about 300 pounds then and had very long hair and a tremendous black shock of a beard. The local newspaper had actually written after describing Cam that "he appeared in court in a business suit", as though he were a gorilla.

After an arduous weeklong "jury trial" (the jury consisting of officers and none of Richard's peers, enlisted men), Richard was convicted, given a Dishonorable Discharge and sent to Leavenworth prison for two years. Like so many of the draft resisters and GI's, Richard Chase listened to his own conscience and simply refused to do what he deeply believed was wrong.

This seed grows today as again, we have seen our country press the poorest citizens onto foreign battlefields without justification where they kill and many of them die. If they say no, as many have already, I hope there are lawyers to stand with them, to put their hands on the shoulders of their clients and say to the jury, as Kunstler did in the Wounded Knee trial of Russell Means and Dennis Banks (American Indian Movement leaders): take good care of these men, "they are my brothers".

One drunken night in early 1970, Ed Polk, an old friend and radical lawyer who had gotten himself named Director of Dallas Legal Services Project, called with an offer I couldn't refuse. He called to offer me the position of head of the elite Law Reform Unit at DLSP. In theory, this unit was exempt from the drudgework of divorce, child custody, and welfare cases. The lawyers of the unit got to do the cream of legal services cases, those cases (often class actions) that would achieve reform of the law and bring social change for a large part of our client community, the poor.

There were four of us in this unit. I thought of all of us as radical lawyers, much more associated with the Movement than with traditional liberalism, veterans of anti-war and civil rights activism and legal services programs that had been part of the War on Poverty. Ready to use the considerable budget of DLSP to bring about big changes.

In the end it went badly as the practical realities (if that's what they were) caused our boss and old friend Ed Polk to curb our zeal and our freedom to lambaste the Dallas establishment with major legal onslaughts. It was for me a period when I got in touch with the legions of Movement folks in the place where I grew up.

The fabled "Lee Park Massacree" occurred during that time, an event where hundreds of Dallas cops, many on horseback, assaulted hundreds of "hippies" (as the Dallas News said of all the people in the park). It was never clear to me why the cops felt there was a need for this. Maybe they thought we were "occupying" this public park and might do what was done in People's Park in Berkeley. Or that dope was being smoked (God forbid!). Or that there was going to be public nudity which would lead to orgies. Or that a public park was no place for people to congregate.

Whatever evil vision we conjured up, the Dallas establishment sent in the troops. The usual injuries, physical and legal, were inflicted on the people as the cops gave vent to their fear and insecurity with nightsticks and random arrests. Sort of a miniature, if less violent, 1968 Democratic Convention in Chicago. The mere presence of longhaired, counter-culture dissenters was somehow a clear and present danger. We hoped we were just that.

In truth we were more likely "the Woodstock nation," in the phrase of the song recorded by Crosby, Stills, Nash and Young, written by Joni Mitchell. This song was the music that followed me from bar to bar that spring and summer. There always seems to be music.

At DLSP the Law Reform Unit was made up of young lawyers: Doug Larson, who became my main buddy in DLSP and a good friend until his death in 2006; Bill Barbisch and Sylvia Demarest—all good lawyers. We mounted significant lawsuits on behalf of poor folk and we had a blast doing it.

Leaving Austin behind in 1970, if only for a few months, meant no main squeeze, a fate I seemed to regard as worse than death. My girlfriend in Austin was letting go after a summer of fun and games at my Lake Travis retreat, a place I had rented in 1969 to do the writing I always wanted to do, though I actually wound up playing away the summer.

I had met Sadie at the legendary Split Rail Inn in Austin one fabulous fall evening and we wound up in her bed. The affair went on in a ragged, up and down course until it ended in the action packed summer of 1970 as I moved to Dallas. It had been good with Sadie in many ways, lots of fun but way too many games.

Initially in Dallas that spring, I knew no women. Early on one of the other lawyers in our unit referred me to a friend of his who had a vacant apartment across from her own. I called her up to see about looking at the vacant apartment. Her name was Suzanne Allen and she invited me over. That very night we became lovers, and so, of course, I took the apartment, having solved two problems at once. She was a waif lost in the big city, very attractive, blonde, slender with a look in her eyes I associated in my mind with someone in the 1920's Paris of Hemingway's imagination. She was actually unsophisticated and this was an asset, not a liability. There were no mind games to deal with.

I think she was anorexic before it was fashionable. This fit well with me because food was always the last thing on my mind–booze and sex tied for the first.

She saw very soon that I drank too much, took crazy chances personally, politically and professionally. I thought these qualities (or character defects) would appall and repulse her but she was actually quite taken with them, which meant there would be no pressure to reform. We quickly became constant companions, skipping work, drinking away days and nights, (she drank little herself but accepted my romanticization of my drinking), puffing marijuana with hippie friends who hung around my tiny apartment a block from Lee Park.

We had two apartments, hers and mine, separated only by a small hallway. Unless it was too full of guests, passers-through or meetings, we lived in my apartment. The manager of the complex consisting of two four-plex buildings, was a gargoyle of a woman who actually made unannounced raids of the premises to be sure there was no hanky-panky going on. She reminded me of H.L. Mencken's definition of a puritan: someone with the haunting fear that someone somewhere might be happy. She never caught Suzanne and me as we hanky-pankyed our days away in the belief that being high and getting laid were the highest states one could experience.

We lay around listening endlessly to Richard and Mimi Fariña records of mine that I loved. My unpredictable companion surprised me often. For example, Suzanne identified with the song "The Falcon" and just as odd was my own longtime passion for the song "Bold Marauder." Both these songs are dark hymns to different forms of evil set to a soft jangling of guitar and dulcimer chords. But our ideals were lofty, as always, even though Suzanne's politics were not well developed. She was a social worker and had her heart in the right place.

When my friend Greg Olds, then editor-in-chief of the Texas Observer, wrote a front-page editorial in the Observer titled "Twentieth Century Heroes" in which he mentioned some radical and alternative progressives and pointed to what they were doing with their lives, he mentioned me. I valued the opinions of both the Texas Observer and Greg very much. For my 31st birthday Suzanne gave me a medallion engraved on one side with a peace symbol and on the other side the inscription "Twentieth Century Hero." I still have it.

She could bowl me over with things like that, connecting with and furthering things I wanted to do or be. I believed I had feelings for her that went beyond lust in those mixed-up hemp-hazy, long Dallas days. We clung to each other within our own world and kept the real world outside even though I was (sometimes) busy being a twentieth century hero by day and a bold marauder by night, at least in my own mind.

It was a time rich with meaning, personal and political struggles, and–always–boozy lovemaking. Although we had two apartments at our disposal when not being raided, she loved to do it in the moving car. She was very good at what she liked to do and it seemed I had a perpetual erection causing her to personify the organ as Eveready and describe it with colorful descriptions–it was the "heart-shaped mushroom". I could tell she had never before been so free in indulging her sexual side; it was highly titillating to me.

Now and then we ventured out of our compound. Once I took her to a party at DLSP offices where she wore peace symbol earrings I gave her. (Remember the symbol was not then ubiquitous and co-opted by every imaginable business.) I could easily see that she caught the eye of the male attorneys and I felt proud that she chose me to be crazy with.

We had made no solemn commitment to each other. It was a day-to-day and, specifically, today kind of thing with us. She delighted me almost daily but eventually my libido led me to other women, or actually one other Dallas woman and Sadie visiting from Austin and creating a scene. Nevertheless, Suzanne tolerated that and stayed with me while I was at DLSP.

It was during this period that I probably smoked more marihuana than any other time. It was readily available; Suzanne liked it better than hooch. But I never was addicted to or even that fond of any of the illegal substances, only the legal one, alcohol. I felt about marihuana the way Maury Maverick did. He said of it: "It just makes me more confused than I already am."

Boarding the Saab (which I called Movement One) and leaving Dallas again in late summer, I already missed Suzanne but I had no idea I'd never see her again.

"It's Good To Fight'em"

She is a dog but here in my home office she's a quadralegal. We don't do a lot of legal business. Now after the dawn of the 21st century Molly and I contemplate the past.

Organizing the Radical Lawyers Caucus and suing the State Bar of Texas in 1970 for excluding the Caucus from the state convention was another of the times it all seemed meaningful and exciting. One reason we could take the legal offensive so often or invoke constitutional rights for our dissident clients was directly traceable to the great Warren court and the many viable avenues of redress it opened to the people of this country. I doubt that there has ever been a time in this country when the practice of law by progressive lawyers was more exciting or productive.

The courts (especially the federal courts) were actually vindicating the rights given us by the revolutionaries we call the Founding Fathers. The Warren court had struck its historic bold blow for the end of school segregation by race in 1954. The salutary effects of this amazing court, as well as courts like the Fifth Circuit Court of Appeals–a bastion of liberal decisions during the civil rights struggles–were felt well into the '70s and even the '80s. Not legislating, as the bellicose Rush Limbaugh's would have it, but carrying out the Bill of Rights, a living document only when courts will protect the rights given to the people.

But the devastating effects of 12 years of Republican federal court appointments from 1980-1992 reversed this situation and created the opposite atmosphere, one that was stultifying. It got worse and worse with appointments like William Rehnquist as Chief Justice. From Earl Warren to William Rehnquist personified the descent of the federal judiciary into the Dark Age. By the mid '80s we were toiling in arid and hostile fields. Many of us were longing for emancipation from legal work, more creative outlets for our energies and visions. A bad situation got a lot worse later with the two Bush presidencies. Rehnquist looked almost human compared to Scalia and Thomas.

There were groups of young Movement lawyers in Dallas and Houston by 1970 in addition to Austin. About 15 of us organized a rump faction of the State Bar of Texas, which we dubbed the Radical Lawyers Caucus. We submitted an ad for the Texas Bar Journal to run prior to the 1970 State Bar Convention in San Antonio. The State Bar (not being well versed in constitutional law)rejected it. The reasons they stated ranged from pretextual to imaginary.

We sued the bar in federal court, which ruled that their action violated our First Amendment rights. It was my great pleasure to try the case before Judge Jack Roberts, a judge we called "the Toad" outside his hearing, and who was no flame-throwing liberal. But he had been appointed by a Democrat, Lyndon Johnson, and was not willing to ignore the First Amendment, even for the legal establishment of Texas. This even though the State Bar was represented by one of the most powerful lawyers in America, Donald Thomas, also said to be LBJ's personal lawyer and a close personal friend of Judge Roberts. In retrospect, the judge seems like a benevolent, fair and compassionate judge.

At the time we thought of Judge Roberts as gruff and unready to entertain our aggressive suits under the magic and mighty Section 1983 of Title 42 U.S. Code, as expanded by the historic Dombrowski v. Pfister case in 1965. For at least 15 years after it was decided by the U.S. Supreme Court, Dombrowski was the vehicle for vindicating the constitutional rights of many people and civil rights groups. The case became the target of the ersatz conservative (the early neo-cons) hatchet men seeking to close the door to the federal courthouse to the riff-raff daring to sue the government, or worse, big corporations (a trickier feat under 1983). Their money and frontal attack brought such suits to a trickle by the end of the 20th century.

The Radical Lawyers Caucus also sought inside status, to be allowed to hold meetings and reach out to our fellow barristers inside that 1970 convention. No soap, said the State Bar again. There was no time to sue.

So we set up shop outside the convention in a suite at the historic Menger Hotel, literally next door to the Alamo, which was appropriate. In the gazebo in front of the Alamo, New York radical lawyer Bill Kunstler gave our keynote speech, with opening talks by our veteran Texas progressive legal heroes, Maury Maverick, Jr. and Warren Burnett.

The day before at Mario's Restaurant, speaking only to a group of lawyers, Kunstler had stunned the regular lawyers and brought tears to the eyes of those of us from the Radical Lawyers Caucus with his powerful call to reject the road to fascism and welcome a new freedom for all. I recently found a tape recording of Kunstler's speeches and donated it to the William Moses Kunstler Fund for Racial Justice, established after Kunstler died in 1995.

We had been a presence at the convention and it trumpeted our arrival on the legal scene in Texas to the dismay of the staid minions of the legal profession. The following year the Individual Rights and Responsibilities Section of the State Bar of Texas was formed under the wily leadership of liberal labor lawyer David Richards. Even in the then arch conservative state bar organization, the IRR Section sailed through its organizing and sanctioning process, the only controversy coming at the convention in 1971, when my law partner Cam Cunningham moved to strike "and Responsibilities" from the name of the Section. That motion failed but in 1972 Dave turned the whole organization over to us radicals (leaving the country for a trip to Europe during the state convention, avoiding the ire of the bar leaders).

The State Bar was horrified as every year since then the IRR Section has invited speakers to its convention program such as Fidel Castro (who has not accepted–yet). One year Margo St. James of the prostitutes "union" COYOTE (Call Off Your Old Tired Ethics) spoke. Kunstler was invited several times as well as the dean of radical lawyers, Arthur Kinoy, and Michael Stepanian, allegedly Hunter Thompson's lawyer as depicted in "Fear and Loathing in Las Vegas". Also, the best federal judge in Texas, William Wayne Justice–one of the more sober occasions, which made it unique.

In late 1970, Brady Coleman was practicing in a personal injury firm in Longview, Texas, when personal events in his life and a desire for more meaningful legal work caused him to put an ad in the Texas Observer, which Cam and I responded to and he joined the firm. Brady added a great dimension to the firm as a lawyer and a person. He possesses an equanimity and good will that causes everybody to like him. He had more trial experience and was able to handle workman's compensation and tort cases, which we had only dabbled in before. Much of what I learned about these cases in my four decades of law, I learned from Brady in the 20 years we practiced law together.

We were prone to saying that we were Movement people first, lawyers second (but in truth, for me, lawyer was not second; it was way down the list). We wanted to use our skills and training as lawyers to advance the cause, in a large sense, and to protect and succor the oppressed, in a singular sense. Our heroes were not Brandeis, Holmes, John Marshall, even Abe Lincoln, as much as they were Clarence Darrow, Charles Garry, Bill Kunstler, Arthur Kinoy, Leonard Boudin–the fighters for social and individual justice, sometimes one client at a time, sometimes sweeping class actions.

We spurned the mystique of our profession and the professionalism that kept us apart from our clients, the people. We looked for new models of doing legal work and found the old reliable one–commune. So we became a commune with distinctly unlawyerly principles: income limitation, communal decisions and full democracy within the office, pro bono work for our "political" clients. We agreed not to draw from the firm's coffers more than we needed to subsist. If there was money left over (not a problem, as a rule) we donated it to other alternative entities such as the local underground newspaper, the Rag, or the free school, Greenbriar.

My partners in this endeavor were Cameron Cunningham and Brady Coleman, at first, and then joining us, John Howard, Bobby Jane Nelson, Bill Schieffelin, Steve Russell and Vivian Mahlab–all lawyers. We had some crackerjack legal workers, none more colorful than Vernell Pratt (purveyor of that famous aphorism: the only sin is frettin'). Julie Howell started as our first legal worker and went on to become a lawyer herself. The legal workers and law clerks over a period of seven or eight years were numerous.

This was no conventional law firm. Doing legal work was not all we did together. We partied hard with the aid of alcohol and a lot of other drugs, or many times just high on what we were doing.

From Clarence Darrow to Bill Kunstler, there was inspiration aplenty. Above all, there was the defining event of our generation: The war in Viet Nam. The war galvanized an entire generation to question all the old saws of our society: of education, religion, family–everything. It was the dawning of the Age of Aquarius, and the mantra was: if it feels good, do it. We did it, and everything, to excess. We were blissfully unaware that we lived at the cultural zenith of our times.

Over the years, I had a lot of fun with some true Movement cases. In spring 1971, John Mitchell, Nixon's Attorney General, was invited to speak at SMU in Dallas, which prompted the Student Mobilization Committee on campus to organize a protest. The war in Viet Nam was still being waged by the Administration Mitchell was part of. The Mobe sought a permit from the university to hold its own conclave with famed Movement lawyer Arthur Kinoy and Chicago 7 defendant John Froines to speak. Predictably, SMU declined to grant the Mobe's permit.

The great young lawyers at the progressive Dallas Legal Services Project (DLSP), headed by my friend and former boss Ed Polk, drafted a suit against SMU. (In 1970, I had taken a leave of absence from the Austin firm to work in the DLSP.) Ed and my other friends and fellow lawyers, Doug Larson, Jim Johnston, Bill Barbisch, Tom Dixon and Ed Cloutman, called me to try the suit in federal court against SMU, one of my alma maters. Under their guidelines, DLSP could not officially represent the Mobe but they did yeomen's service in drafting pleadings and briefs for this case. The night before the trial I drove to Dallas to work through the night getting ready to try the case in federal court.

I spoke by phone with Kinoy in New York, who not only helped us immeasurably with the law, being a real scholar, but he also gave pep talks about how good it was to fight 'em. This erudite little man was a treasure of the national legal community. Like Kunstler, Ben Smith, Morty Stavis–so many of the great lawyers of the Movement–Kinoy is no longer alive. I feel lucky to have had the opportunity to work with him. The week we battled in court in April was one of the most truly memorable of any time of the past four decades I've done this work.

Kinoy and Froines came to Dallas and we all gathered together at DLSP offices and homes to strategize the on-going legal fight which went from federal to state court, from our seeking an injunction against SMU in federal court, to defending against their suit in state court to enjoin my clients from some mysterious behavior that was very vague. In fact, not only was the behavior to be enjoined vague, but also to whom the injunction might apply was equally vague. A judge neatly in the hip pocket of one of Dallas' most prestigious firm of "rug lawyers"–as we called the big, rich firms, representing SMU–granted an entirely meaningless and unenforceable injunction against my client.

I averaged three or four hours sleep at night and, even with all the beer and marihuana I could take, I was on an adrenaline high the whole week. The camaraderie, solidarity and exhaustion were like a catharsis. We lost the legal battles of that week but won the war in the long run. It had been good to fight 'em.

I doubt that SMU is proud of having John Mitchell inside dedicating its new law library (or whatever it was,) while the distinguished Arthur Kinoy had to speak outside on the main mall where about two-thirds of the progressive lawyers in Texas were assembled (most of us about 30 years old). The empty state court injunction did not keep us from assembling on the SMU campus nor did our suit force SMU to allow us an inside location. The week of media coverage of our political fight in the courts spurred the organizing efforts of the Student Mobilization Committee at the usually soporific campus of SMU.

I was often shooting from the hip, being the bold marauder of the courts, fighting for First Amendment rights to be sure, but mostly for the sisters and brothers of the Movement whose activism made it possible. Kinoy liked to speak of "the people in motion," a people's movement. These students were in motion at that time and place. I had fun being with them, speaking for them in court, battling the power structure (as we had called it back in OEO).

When the week ended, my law partners Brady Coleman and Cam Cunningham came through Dallas to get me, and we were all off to participate in the militant May Day anti-war demonstration in Washington, D.C. We had taken in cash all the money in the firm bank account to go to Washington. It wasn't a lot but all week we flashed the "benjies and grants" to pay for food and, of course, booze. We would be both activists and lawyers that week in the capital when a hundred thousand or more took to the streets to bring the central government to a standstill.

Thousands were rounded up and placed in jail–or, actually, taken to a huge makeshift detention center at RFK Stadium. My partners and I could just as easily have been arrested but we were not, so we performed our role as lawyers, trying to win freedom for our imprisoned comrades. I was personally able to go into a D.C. court and obtain the release of Alice Embree, one of the smartest and most prominent activists in the Movement community in Austin.

A night later I remember going with Cam and Brady to RFK where we went through the catacombs of makeshift cells, tents really, searching in vain for any of the incarcerated people from Texas. It was eerie, reminiscent of the stadia in Central America where brutal despots detained those who would be "disappeared". (Now Guantanamo has taken it further into the dark side of tyranny.) Later, the government paid damages for these bad faith arrests, made without regard to specific criminal conduct, without probable cause, seeking only to round-up as many as possible and bust them, a patently unconstitutional tactic.

It was periods like this, filled with action, that gave vitality and dynamism to my life in those times. As to the law and running a firm, we were making it up as we went along. We were about as far from what law firms were like in that time as we could be. Our own lives were about as far from those of our parents, aunts and uncles, even our siblings, as we could get.

But there was a Movement community nationwide, much more than the "Woodstock nation" as Joni Mitchell wrote of in her immortal song. We had a strong sense of belonging to the community, from the lawyers organizing in the National Lawyers Guild and Southern Legal Action Movement, to peoples' groups like SDS, SNCC, VVAW, even unorganized counter-culture pockets like Hippies and Yippies, from Haight-Ashbury to Greenwich Village. There was no doubt in our minds that we were going to change the world. And we did, though not nearly as much as we thought we would.

I always had a special feeling for cases involving First Amendment rights. There were also many criminal cases, a lot of which involved Fourth Amendment rights against unreasonable search and seizure. At one point in the '70s I was going to New Orleans every two months on average to argue civil cases involving free speech rights or suits to obtain conscientious objector (CO) status or criminal cases with search issues before the Fifth Circuit Court of Appeals. Like Ben Smith, a Center for Constitutional Rights lawyer I knew who lived in New Orleans, I was not well suited for the environs of the French Quarter. If you have a drinking problem, I don't recommend New Orleans.

In 1972 we sued the University of Texas because they denied use of university facilities for the National Lawyers Guild Convention to be held in 1973. It was one of several big cases I tried with assistance from John Howard after his licensure in late 1972.

In the trial, we were up against a well-known, high-up lawyer in the UT System General Counsel's Office. He was a guy who was especially supercilious. We knew we probably could not persuade Judge Roberts to go with our side and force the University to let us have the convention there. But the UT System lawyer was getting on our nerves such that back at counsel tables, well out of the hearing of the judge (who was hard of hearing anyway), when we handed this lawyer exhibits to look at, we were quietly saying "there you go, fucknose". This infuriated the haughty lawyer but he was not willing to whine and tattle to the judge. Even in difficult cases, you must try to have some fun.

The appeal of the case came up for argument in New Orleans and it was the first and only time I had to beg off argument in an appearance before the Fifth Circuit or any other court because of drinking. Nancy had gone with me to New Orleans early, and we had several days to carouse in the French Quarter. I wound up too physically sick (ulcer, gastritis, whatever) to appear in court and was allowed to file a short brief later in addition to the appeal brief already on file. We lost. Certainly, this was no fun.

Most of the time, if I was sick or badly hung over, I gutted it up and went to court. In the 16 years I was a drunk practicing law I never appeared in court under the influence of the elixir unless it was the morning after hangover. I figured that didn't count.

In the summer of 1971, the historic National Lawyers Guild national convention was held in Boulder, Colorado. All three of our lawyers–Brady, Cam and I– and our law clerk, John Howard, went. Other Texas lawyers were out there, including Larry Daves and Larry Sauer. It was at this wild convention that the divided NLG voted after hot debate to admit law students and jailhouse lawyers to membership, which our Texas group voted for.

We had adopted a practice of drinking in various bars until debate was over, when we would show up on the floor of the convention and cast all the Texas delegation votes–to the great chagrin of one older lawyer from Houston who kept trying to track us down, as he apparently had different views. He never did, but we decided that there were two factions in the Texas delegation. We were the Armadillo faction and this one older guy was the Dogshit faction. The crowning blow was when I was elected by the prevailing Armadillo faction as regional vice-president from the Southwest.

One night of the convention we had a party of the Armadillos on a mountain somewhere near Boulder. After much to drink and smoke, I attempted to drive down the mountain in my trusty Saab with my wife Helen and Cam in the car. They tell me I came within a twigs breath of plunging the car off the mountainside and killing us all. In several years of drinking with Cam it was the only time I ever saw him throw up. Helen said he was pale from fear, nor was she any better.

I was the only one who had taken a room at a motel or hotel and virtually everybody in the Texas delegation (Armadillo faction) slept there every night, wall to wall people. It was a revelation each foggy morning to see who you would wake up next to or in what state of undress. No one asked any questions.

It reminded me a little of Kunstler telling me that over the months of trial in the Chicago 7 case in Chicago, it was not unusual at night in bed to be making love and not even know who your partner was. Remember: he loved his clients. But I don't mean to be derisive. I expect he exaggerated the sexual aspect and I'm pretty sure that in our room at Boulder few would have been conscious enough for amor.

In 1971 another auspicious bit of litigation came our way when the telephone company screwed up my lawyer listing in the telephone directory. Of course, I immediately retained my law partner Brady Coleman to go after these corporate bunglers. As we pressed a claim for damages against Southwestern Bell, I was contacted by Jon Dee Lawrence, counsel for Ma Bell. I viewed this as a salutary turn of events since he was a fellow I knew from a crazy time in a summer gone by when as college students he, George Schell and I attempted to sell big, glossy, color-illustrated family Bibles in Grand Rapids, Michigan.

One day I had talked a young, poor family who lived in a trailer into buying the expensive book. Hearing more of their situation, I then proceeded to talk them out of spending the money on this big slick good book. At that point, only a couple of weeks into the summer, I knew I was through as a family Bible salesman. George and Jon Dee reached the same conclusion and we gave it up. Later, at UT, Jon Dee helped me get a job at Scottish Rite Dormitory for women washing dishes at the dining room for meals and I was damn glad to get it.

Now my old bible-selling buddy was calling me because he was a lawyer for Southwestern Bell. I could definitely pick up the scent of a settlement of the big case. Our suit against Southwestern Bell resulted in an out-of-court settlement for the princely sum of $500.00 (a lot more money then than it is now, still probably the "nuisance value" the insurance adjusters speak of with contempt).

We put it all into a massive party at Lake Austin over Labor Day weekend which we called "The Last Annual Ma Bell Counter Rip-Off Wild Boar Feast." A huge number of chickens were roasted, kegs of beer and live music provided by the Soeur Queens, an all woman group. We had to rent a generator to accomodate electric instruments and amplification. I still believe it was the best party ever in a town legendary for its parties.

It was the only time I ever took acid. I spent the whole weekend partying and one long, euphoric night in a makeshift bed–a blanket on the ground–outside under the stars with two women simultaneously. I met these two close friends that night and made love with one and then the other by turns. Sometimes we all just cuddled though I don't believe anyone slept. I recall running in circles around our amorous encampment in the sultry night air yelling as loud as I could "I want to live forever!"

Both of these women are still good friends of mine although they have moved out of the state. It was the party of parties, though by the next morning, a workday, I definitely did not want to live forever.

I can't say honestly that I regret such evenings, because at that age rapacious appetites drove me to such hedonism and I loved the doing of it. I did not see any moral issues about this but it turned out there were health issues for me in partying all-out, mostly about drinking. It was at once something I could not control and something in which I knowingly egged myself on to more and greater excesses.

In the Deep

Life boils down to its essentials for Molly. She has infirmities though, including liver problems. She is 18 years old.

The sixties lasted into the mid '70s around Austin. I have publicly stated that I was in a blackout for the entire '70s and it is not such a great exaggeration.

Some truly remarkable things happened: mostly bad, but some miraculously good. My mother became ill with a degenerative brain disease and the strongest, most self-reliant person I knew fell to a lowly state where she could not speak and required diapers, constant care, all over a period of a few years. It was the second most heart-breaking experience of my life. I could do nothing; no one could.

For the first three years, I knew nothing of her true condition. I was self-absorbed, engaged completely in my world. In 1973, she came to Austin to the Austin State Hospital where a battery of tests was done and organic brain syndrome was diagnosed. We were told that there was nothing we could do.

A year or two later, after she suffered pronounced losses of capability, it was over except for lying abed for several years unable to do anything at all. We moved her to upstate New York near my sister. As I put her on an air ambulance in the fall of 1975, I knew she would not ever return to Texas alive. Her body was flown back in March 1981 to Cleburne, Texas, where she was born, where my sister and I were born, where so many relatives on both sides of the family have lived out their lives, some still alive.

My mother, Estelle Whitworth Simons, was buried next to my dad. From the age of 53 until her death 10 years later, she had a life seemingly lacking any quality. Everyone's worst nightmare.

Yet, in truth, we do not know what it was like for her. She could not speak or respond to us for the last few years, but how strongly she clung to that minimal stage of life. Always perseverant, she hung on and we don't really know what was going on in her brain.

I don't even know what medications, if any, she received after leaving Texas. While here, she got at one time or another every psychotropic drug that was in use legally in this country. Indeed, sometime between her collapse of 1970 and her coming to Austin State Hospital in 1973, she had been subjected to electroshock treatment. I had not known about it at the time. It is still hard for me to imagine my mother in the throes of a depression, but apparently, she was. At least in part, it was probably the result of her damaged brain deteriorating.

I was too personally embroiled in my drinking life and the law to take enough care of her. Also, my first marriage was unraveling. And I had fallen in love and lost the woman who was the soul mate of lore for me. Together we had lost the only son I fathered. I did not know how much that would hurt in the mature years of life. It was like a land mine waiting just below the surface for me to tread those years ahead. It was, I believe, the same for Nancy.

At the disastrous 1972 bar convention where I stayed drunk on scotch for one week, a Dallas lawyer who was a friend of Suzanne's told me she had died mysteriously on an airplane after a stint with the Hare Krishnas (she was in the throes of some kind of desperation to find some meaning in life). I had not really seen her after the summer of 1970 when I returned to my Austin law collective. Hearing of Suzanne's death for the first time at the convention while in an alcoholic haze capped off the nightmarish experience and sent me homeward and into Seton Hospital. I never learned more about the cause or circumstances of her death. I knew she had branched out from pot, taking other drugs.

There was speculation that drugs brought about her death and I believe that was the cause, one way or another, possibly in conjunction with anorexia. She was still in her mid-20s. I had thought that much of the story of the time in Dallas was all about me; much of it now in my memory is, and will always be, all about her.

In 1972, I spent about five days quaffing scotch without eating during a state bar convention in Houston. A girlfriend had stuck with me on the trip even as she watched the pickling process I was undergoing. Incredibly, night driving to get back home, my VW bug blew its engine at Columbus where a Texaco station night attendant pulled a gun on me when I insisted he could and would fix it. He called the sheriff, too. But across the street a Gulf station (Exxon, today) did take pity on a pathetic drunken driver, or more likely on the attractive woman holding me up. I could drive no further and the VW was dead.

A station employee getting off work gave us a lift to La Grange where Brady Coleman, my law partner, found us hitchhiking. (I had called him with pleas for help from Columbus.) As the sun of a summer morning came up I stood woozily on the highway with a bottle of Green and White Scotch Whiskey in one hand and the other stuck out, thumb pointing skyward. I crawled gratefully into Brady's VW bug and was transported back to Austin where all my sorrows, responsibilities and impending comeuppances awaited me.

It was at this point that Helen, my wife of ten years, finally threw in the towel. She was very tolerant, patient–not to say long-suffering. She could abide no more. I did not blame her. The only question was why it took so long. I was incorrigible beyond redemption. I wound up at Seton Hospital (the old one, dark and with the dread nuns in full habit) drying out, feeling like a dead man, when Jack Whitaker, my friend, my doctor, told me my liver was the size of a basketball.

The day or two I survived between getting back home and being admitted at Seton I had the DT's for the only time I could be pretty sure I had them. Great waves of unbearable anxiety would come rolling over me until I woke nearly screaming (or was I actually screaming?) My fear centered on Eleanor, called Pooh, my 9 year old daughter, the person I loved most in the world. Just as the fear I felt trying to sleep in 1956 above that funeral parlor in Muskogee focused on my mother, in my delirium of 1972 it fixed on my little girl. Never in my life have I suffered sheer terror to such a degree. It was palpable, burning my mind with the intensity of it.

That was a state of consciousness I have never experienced except in delirium tremens. I was truly near convulsions and the last sayonara. Somewhere in the surreal mists in the wake of flashing terror, I called a friend and was rescued, only temporarily, by being driven around while I tipped up the beautiful green bottle of salvation, a most welcome white wine. The elixir delivered me for a few hours from the blinding fear and crashing dread on an Austin summer night.

I was in the hospital for about five days. Jack told me not to touch a drop for at least 90 days to give my liver a fighting chance to regenerate. I made 30 days with no drinking, 30 more drinking moderately and the last 30 back in the saddle again going at my normal rate.

The '70s was a decade I've always claimed to have been in a blackout the whole decade but I also had arguably the most important cases and victories of my decades as a lawyer. The drinking brought me crashing down. But other things, wonderful, near miraculous things happened. God loves a rummy; it must be so.

The most miraculous and wonderful thing was the most unexpected. I got Nancy back against all odds. I thought I had lost her forever. As I convalesced at home in August of 1972, I got a call from Nancy in Denver.

I was a defeated wretch, worried about being without my daughter. It had been my love of my daughter that made it impossible for me to do what I should have done 8 years earlier to keep Nancy (and our son). I had a deep love for my little blond daughter. In California, where Nancy and I fled in summer of 1964 for her to have the baby and for her and me to start over, I could not get the image of my daughter Eleanor, Pooh as she was known then, out of my mind.

That billboard advertising sunscreen that Jody Foster posed for was all over Northern California. It showed a girl about Pooh's age, two or three. That infernal billboard of the beautiful child haunted me, as I feared life not seeing my daughter grow up.

Nancy and I had taken a small, cheap apartment in Berkeley. It would be 6 months before our son was born and it would not be in California but in Dallas when I could do nothing, or felt I could do nothing to keep from losing him and I had already lost Nancy. The choices I made were bad and the opposite choices would have been bad.

The way things were in my final semester in law school was terrible but we went on from there, Helen and I with our little daughter. For a while there were better times, mostly our time living in Houston. By August of '72, back in Austin, I thought I had hit rock bottom. Helen was through trying to hold together a marriage not meant to be.

I was reinvigorated by hearing from Nancy. I am not quite sure why she called; I thought she had given up on me. She had married in 1970 but the marriage was breaking up. There was, as we talked on the phone, a mutual desire to see each other again–somewhere away from our respective homes. We devised a plan to meet in Taos, New Mexico.

It was exciting to see her again and we spent the first night in Santa Fe at the La Fonda. After a snootful of Turquoise Margaritas at the bar on our first night, we were back into remonstrance filled with guilt and blame. Apparently, we needed to get that out of our systems. As though to remove ourselves from all that, we proceeded to Taos and the Taos Inn. The rest of the week in Taos was magical as it had been with us before. At the end of a week, I boarded a plane to return to Texas.

In my heart I knew we were not destined to be apart. Back in Austin and Denver we wrote, something we had always done. Through our letters, we agreed we needed to be together. But it actually happened only because of Nancy's courage in taking a risk moving to Austin. There had been no more of the promises that were not kept before. All we agreed to was that we loved each other and we wanted to be together.

On October 2, 1972, she arrived in the Volvo station wagon packed with all that she cared to have with her. I had already rented the tiny apartment we called Little Bit of Taos across from the Elisabet Ney Museum in Hyde Park. On that day our lives joined together for life. Improbable as all hell, it was. A miracle, it seemed.

In 1972, it was still the sixties in Austin; virtually anything seemed possible. I had gone from the bottom to the top in only a few weeks sandwiched around that fateful week in Taos. Life was suddenly too grand for words, after I nearly was killed or died of alcohol poisoning the long dark night on the highway back from Houston following my binge of binges.

The turnaround was dizzying. Celebration was called for: drinks all around. That day I met Nancy at a place then called Mrs. Robinson's near my law office when she rolled in. It was a bar primarily, what else? We had some beers and moved on to a place then called The Oyster Bar, which was next to the Capitol. We had real drinks and some food, New Orleans style, oysters, shrimp. We went home to spend the first night of the rest of our lives together.

I tried to be cool. I was hesitant for her to see how deeply I loved her and needed her or to see me as mawkish or clinging. I always remember my dad as he was at the end. The ghost image of my father's great need of my mother came to me again. But inside I was the 4th of July. A rather large, quality joint she had brought from Denver sent us hungrily to bed touching, teasing, tasting, totally enmeshed as if it was the first time.

As time went by, I came to know that I had never been more in love. In fact, I had never been truly in love with anyone else. This was genuine. The intense light we reflected together so far outshone all other amorous feelings I'd had for anyone that they all paled into insignificance. Holding Nancy in the tiny adobe-like apartment on a bed we did not even own wrapped me in a spell like no other. It had always been like that from day one. It was instantaneous, all-consuming, the light of the borealis, all nerve endings transmitting pure pleasure to the brain and the brain messaging pure longing.

Cases

In the quiet of the ville, Molly tires of probate cases we are trying to clear. She asks me with a twinkle in her eye to tell about the cases again. I start to recall.

I have always considered fun to be a major requirement for legal cases and too often it is just the opposite. We can look back with pride or pleasure sometimes. In the throes of trying cases, one would hardly ever stop and think: Damn, this is fun. Yet, it does happen. Over the years, there have been more than I expected. For me the Roky Erickson case comes to mind.

Roky is a slightly mad musical genius who in the late '60s started Austin's first psychedelic rock band, the 13th Floor Elevators, and it has become a legend. He was the whole package: long hair, wild eyes, stoned out. But he is also a sensitive and creative person, the type of person who does not set out to achieve fame; it chases him. And people who don't like what Roky is are prone to chase him, too.

When he got caught with drugs–marihuana–in about 1969, a high-powered, perhaps well-meaning lawyer pled insanity. Specifically, incompetence to stand trial. The result was imprisonment in the infamously grim Rusk State Hospital in East Texas.

This is, or was, in effect, an indeterminate sentence since the only way to get out was for the bull-goose shrink to certify you as sane. (Even then it was necessary to get a jury trial and court judgment.) But, of course, none of the Dr. Strangelove shrinks out at Rusk would go out on a limb and recommend release. So Roky wasted away in a world made weird by a bucket of psychiatric drugs (far worse than the relatively harmless weed he had been using for weird). There seemed to be no hope he would ever be released.

In late 1970, his brother Mike hired me to try to spring the already legendary counter-culture icon from the dark dungeon that was Rusk. The doctors at Rusk would only say two things: Roky's prognosis was "guarded" and they could not say with reasonable medical certainty that he would not go back to using drugs if he were released. As though that would be enough to hold him indefinitely.

Our firm was starting to look like it could be our day jobs, like we might actually make a living from practicing law the way we did. All kinds of people in the Austin counter-culture (second only to the Haight-Ashbury, surely) called and brought us their legal business. In times of hardship, there were benefits held at the fabulous underground venues of the era,

Armadillo World Headquarters, Soap Creek Saloon, Vulcan Gas Company, the One Knight. It seemed we were part of a true community and the people of that community wanted us to stay around. We were lawyers for the counter-culture as well as the politically radical activists.

To be Roky's lawyer was to be a celebrity myself. The engine that drives a trial lawyer is ego and mine was getting juiced big time.

It took two years to get to a jury trial, much of the time our own case-building and preparation. We had to find, hire and work with shrinks, who had to see Roky at Rusk, give him the MMPI and such tests, write their reports.

We hired two very good psychiatrists; one was the local Dick Alexander, my choice for MVP, most valuable psychiatrist. The other was an avant garde teacher at the University of California-Davis whose credentials were great, as were his theories. But it was the local Dr. Alexander who was on the jury's wavelength. We also hired a psychologist for testing and testifying. With these expert witnesses primed and paid, we had only to prepare Roky himself to testify.

John Howard clerked for our firm and became very interested in Roky and his case. He wrote a long, comprehensive paper as a senior law student about Rusk State Hospital and indirectly, Roky Erickson. John had only been licensed for a month before the trial, at which he both sat as second chair and testified, based on his trips to Rusk to see Roky. He did a masterful job of working with Roky and preparing him to testify.

The old saw among the courthouse regulars is that a lawyer should never get emotionally involved with his case. Our approach in cases that were more than routine was to become emotionally involved. As Kunstler said, he loved his clients. A lawyer who loves his client can surpass his own limitations and achieve miraculous things. It is more than simply caring what happens to the client. It is law with a passion.

Both John and I were in this mode in Roky's case, perhaps for different reasons. For John it was a personal feeling for Roky and it enabled him to do extraordinary work leading up to the trial. For reasons of my own, I was enabled to do extraordinary work in the trial of the case in one of the most extraordinary weeks of my life.

We were able to get a jury trial the week after Thanksgiving 1972. As a rule, the prosecutor assigned to the particular trial court tried the cases. For Roky's case the District Attorney himself, Bob Smith, tried the case. He was a surly trial lawyer (though we later became friends, as we were, alas, both alcoholics sober in AA). He had contempt for hippies, regarded Roky's music as loud madness and clearly disdained our law firm.

The trial had gone well; it pays to be prepared. Arguing the case to the jury, I read lines of poetry written by the client and spoke loftily of his musical genius. I knew I was on a roll and having fun. We had picked a good jury. It was one (maybe the only one I've ever had) of those cases when the jury could have decided without deliberating, just agreeing there in the jury box. They were out 5 minutes, barely long enough to elect a foreman. Standing before the judge as we received that verdict and realized that Roky was now free, I felt maybe the most exultant moment of my life in the courtroom. It was transcendent, a high unapproached by any chemical uplift I ever experienced. All the doubts and anguish over all the years I battled with being a lawyer came into clear focus and the certainty that I had done what I was meant to do crystallized in that few seconds. I've never felt anything like it before or since. But, alas, it lasted only seconds.

A burly bailiff was standing in the doorway to the court summoning me to appear in another criminal court for another jury trial to start, as they say, instanter. It was only the largest quantity marihuana case ever tried in Travis County to that time. Purely a criminal case. But one I would have chosen to try some other time than that particular week. It had been set for trial by the judge in the other of our two criminal district courts in what was an effort of at least one of our criminal district judges to ambush me in retaliation for a civil rights suit in which I had named the judges as defendants–admittedly an audacious tactic prompted by political reasons, and a long shot to succeed.

I went straight to the other courtroom without lunch and immediately started the voir dire, and was off and running in the second big jury trial of the week after Thanksgiving 1972. Aside from an illegal search and seizure, we had little to work with, but again we were atypically blessed: we got a good jury.

I was only 33 years old but that week would turn out to be the high-water mark of my performance as a trial lawyer, as we also won that case. I really knew I was having fun then. I could practically hear the blasts of yon triumphant trumpets sounding a hero's march. I thought I had finally hit a mark I was capable of performing at and would continue from there. But the truth is I never hit that mark again– victorious in two difficult and meaningful jury trials in one week.

I spoke to the great Texas trial lawyer Warren Burnett soon afterwards. He said: "You know, you are as good a lawyer now as you will ever be." He meant it in a complimentary way but I scoffed. I had only just begun and I was headed north, up, up and away. The combination of doing your best, winning and having fun was hard to achieve; I did hit two out of three sometimes, but it did not make me as ecstatic as the November '72 blitzkrieg after which the District Attorney and his top trial lawyer, the illustrious Herman Gotcher, lay in the dust at the OK Corral. Even Cam, the law partner who generally wanted any glory to be his, suggested I do a victory lap at the Travis County Courthouse. I did one, with John, at Scholz' Bier Garten instead.

I think there is a relatively simple, non-legal reason I was sky high and hitting on all cylinders that week. Nancy had come back to live with me in October. We were comfortable in our modest but charming tiny apartment we called Little Bit of Taos. Life was good; hell, life was magical, beyond belief. I was empowered by the happiness of having Nancy at last. I wanted to show her I was the best damned lawyer around. Don't misunderstand; I had worked long and hard on both these cases, especially Roky's; I had strong feelings and that was ample motivation. But the very personal factor was that little extra boost that nudges one into the next level.

Somehow the title of Bud Shrake's novel "Strange Peaches" had become a joke between Nancy and me, only we said "strange acorns" (a way of saying things are weird). Before she came from Denver, I sent her a box of acorns from the park at 41st and Red River where as mere kids, we had made love. These "strange acorns" had become nuggets of gold the week after Thanksgiving in 1972.

Only a few short months before that I had convalesced at the old Seton Hospital, my liver the size of a basketball. My wife had announced the termination of our frail relationship; my girlfriend of the time had gone away to New Mexico, having had it with my drunkenness, and the woman I loved and pined for was married and lived in Denver. It was one of the darkest times of my life.

I had no hope of things improving until, out of the blue, I heard from Nancy, in Denver, who was also divorcing, and we agreed to meet in Taos. It was the re-start of something big. I don't know what would have happened if she had not called. In autumn 1972, I had achieved a pinnacle in my work largely because my life had risen to a crest. It is further confirmation of the inter-relatedness of life and work; as Robert Frost said, they are one.

It is integral to the happenings of that week that I believed so strongly in what we were doing, in the clients. Neither Roky nor the other client, a Hispanic man, deserved to be locked up by this society for many years. Both had gone astray of the law over a relatively harmless substance, marihuana, that I believed–and still believe–should be legal.

In 1973 a very good friend and member of the Austin Movement community was busted at the border in Laredo when a search of her car yielded drug contraband. To make things worse, or more complicated, the car belonged to the wife of one of my law partners. No, we were not engaged in an illegal extra-curricular enterprise. Nor was the partner's wife or even Mary, the one caught at the border. A slick drug dealer had importuned her into making the run and she actually did not even know what she was transporting though she must have known it was some kind of drugs.

She had called us but I got my old law school buddy Warren Weir in San Antonio (which was closer to the border) to handle the case in federal court in Laredo. There was a jury trial and Mary was convicted. She was a much beloved person and maker of good music. To all of us who knew her a prison sentence (I believe it was 2 years) was just unacceptable.

I took on the appeal and worked like a dog on the brief that should have kept her out of jail. It involved Due Process Fifth Amendment and Right to Confront Witnesses Sixth Amendment points and other issues of great importance in criminal cases. It stands out clearly in my mind as the best brief I ever wrote and I was certain we would prevail.

When the argument came around, I learned that the wife (perhaps at that time, the girlfriend) of a friend was the Assistant U.S. Attorney who was appearing for the Government. I stood to begin my argument in the august Fifth Circuit courtroom in New Orleans. Before I could get very far the Senior Judge of the three-judge panel, Griffin Bell of Georgia, interrupted me with a question: Didn't I want to abandon four of my five points on appeal; he focused on the last point in my brief.

It was a good point but so were the other four. And I did not know which point the other two judges on that panel might be moved by. When I declined to abandon 80% of my argument, Judge Bell looked at me with some distaste and asked: "What are you, one of those OEO lawyers?"

The reference was to legal services lawyers (originally funded through OEO, my old employer). It reflected the distaste some establishment types had for legal cases that rocked the boat and for the fearless lawyers at legal services programs nationwide who dared sue the big boys on behalf of the little guys. I suppose it was a measure of how effective these programs, like Dallas Legal Services Project, had been.

But it did not augur well for me that day in New Orleans. In this cavalier manner, the three-judge panel with Judge Bell leading them managed to gloss over the heart of the case and affirm Mary's conviction and prison sentence.

On the plane ride home, I sat with the U.S. Attorney who argued the case against us. After a couple of drinks she admitted that she and her boyfriend or husband, my old friend, had gone over my brief with a fine tooth comb and could not see how I could lose on the arguments. Subsequently, that brief was sharpened even more and the analysis crafted into an absolutely unbeatable legal argument for a Petition for the Writ of Certiorari to the United States Supreme Court. It was clearly the best I had ever or could ever do, yet the Supremes denied cert.

It was a lesson: a bad message. You could be right on the law and still lose. At the age of 35, when I wrote this brief and petition, I assumed my losses (few actually even though I was acting out the role of the drunken trial lawyer) were because the law or the facts were against me or, more likely, I had not done a good enough job with the case. Here was a case where I was right on the law as applied to these facts and I had done the best job of analyzing and writing it that could have been done and I lost the case.

As I said, it wasn't just any case. The client was a special person in our community and I had vowed to keep her out of prison. Was it the beginning of the cynicism that seems to overtake everyone in the justice business?

In 1972, eight Viet Nam Veterans Against the War activists had been indicted in Florida for having conspired to blow up the Republican convention in Miami that year. They became known as the Gainesville Eight. They were represented by the Center for Constitutional Rights in the persons of Morty Stavis, Nancy Stearns and Doris Peterson.

Two of the defendants were from Texas and had been clients of ours, John Kniffin and Bill Patterson; so it was logical for us to represent them. At that time, there were only three partners: Brady Coleman, Cam Cunningham and me. It was clear that one of us would have to stay home and keep the law firm going. It's not important now how it was decided, but Brady and Cam went to Florida and represented the VVAW clients.

Larry Turner, now a judge, was local Florida counsel. The jury trial went on in federal court in Gainesville for a few weeks before all were acquitted. It was a great triumph for the Movement. I was and am proud that Cam and Brady could be in this case and contribute to defending the VVAW clients. We had strong ties to the VVAW, having done other legal work for many of its members, and I had done a lot of it myself.

The trial was in the summer of 1973 and for much of that summer I was the only senior lawyer in the firm back in Austin, trying to manage Cam and Brady's caseloads, and ride herd on a bunch of younger lawyers working in the firm at its old West 15th Street office. These included Bobby Nelson, John Howard, Bill Schieffelin, Bill Kimble and Mike Hudson (who was a law clerk,) as well as other lawyers working out of our office trying to get another firm started headed by Carol Oppenheimer and Gary Cohen. We had a couple of legal workers around–Vernell Pratt and Meg Stone.

With two of the other senior lawyers gone for a good bit of the summer, what started as a joke took hold. Someone had read about Leon Jaworski, of the power firm of Fulbright & Jaworski, being called "Colonel" by the many younger lawyers in that firm. That summer a number of the younger lawyers and legal workers in and around the office started calling me "the Colonel" and most of them still do.

We had some fun that summer while holding down the fort at the old law commune. We became closer than we ever would have if Cam and Brady had been there. It was a consolation to me for not going out to Florida on the Gainesville 8 case.

Perhaps a much larger "consolation" (and a great privilege) came along a year later when John Howard and I were the lawyers from our firm who got to handle the Wounded Knee case. All of us were able to contribute to these important legal cases of the time and that is what we were there for.

Another major component of our caseload related to civil rights. The civil rights movement was the other pillar of our cause.

From the time of the "stand-ins" at Austin movie theaters in 1961, I had been involved in civil rights activism. I believe I filed one of the earliest, if not the first, lawsuit in the Western District of Texas, Austin Division under the 1964 Civil Rights Act's Title VII prohibiting employment discrimination. That case involved racial discrimination and was litigated for 6 years (so favorably settled "on the steps of the courthouse" in 1974 that I had a photograph made of the check).

Other cases over the years involved women's rights, gay rights, prisoners' rights and elder rights. During the '70s especially, my law partner Bobby Nelson and I tried many of these cases in the federal courts. She had several big cases of this nature and did a good job on them.

Title VII cases came in assorted types: discrimination on the basis of race, national origin, gender and age. Bobby and I had all these kinds of job bias cases. But they were, in those days, very difficult cases to prove, in that intent had to be proven. Employers always had some other reason they advanced for firing, demoting and thrusting the client into the shit detail.

One area that was especially tricky was sexual harassment cases. A very quiet, petite and attractive Hispanic woman came to see me after the Equal Employment Opportunity Commission (EEOC) had found "no cause" to believe she had been discriminated against at work because of sexual harassment. At the time Ronald Reagan was President and Clarence Thomas headed up the EEOC, which did an initial administrative investigation. They almost always found no cause. According to them, no one was discriminated against; employers were free to do as they pleased. My client was determined to get justice.

I have to admit I discouraged her because I had seen people invest great time and money in a case only to be severely disappointed. I told her she would be asked at deposition all about her sexual history. She told me (and I totally believed her) she had only had sex with her husband–ever. It is not required but she had virtually no history. She was so embarrassed she neglected to tell me all that she had been subjected to at work from the boss. I reluctantly took the case.

At the deposition of the boss, we got a wake up call. No longer employed by the defendant company, he was free to tell the truth under oath. (In my experience, employers and their lawyers frequently require perjury from employees.) He admitted what amounted to assaulting my client in a storage and file room to the extent of backing her up to a wall, attempting to fondle her and taking his penis out and trying to force her to touch it. A large Hispanic fellow, he was almost proud to tell what he thought showed his machismo .

Needless to say, both defense counsel and I snapped to attention and the dollar value of the case went up exponentially. Showing intent was not a problem. The company quickly settled the case for good bucks.

Had my client not have been determined, this case would not have been filed. It was one of many times that clients educated me. This woman persevered against my advice and she got justice, to the extent possible. It was always important to listen to the client, to leave the final decision to her/him, if at all possible. Often the client is right.

Of course, I also remember trying a race discrimination case in federal court in San Antonio when we were sandbagged mid-trial by a dead-on case the judge happily found allowing him to dismiss the case. Neither I nor defense counsel knew of the case (a district court case that was unreported in the federal reporter system, as are most district trial court cases). I had acceded to the decision of the client to proceed on a case I regarded as weak. The day after the trial was aborted by the judge, she brought a couple of big friends and stormed my office yelling about how I had sold her out, been bought off, etc. It took half an hour to clear them out. I felt bad for her even though I had given it all I had. We probably lost more job discrimination cases than we won. It was never easy to take.

One of mine that I remember was what I called the "Chicken Plucker Case". I represented a Hispanic man who was fired from a chicken processing plant in Gonzales, Texas. Whereas in military cases we had succeeded in teaching our federal judge, Jack Roberts, the law on CO's such that he never ruled against us on one of these, we were not so lucky on the law of employment discrimination. It was just a concept that the judge did not grasp (in this he was far from alone among federal judges). By the time Junior Magallanez was fired as a chicken plucker, I despaired of going before the Toad (the nickname the judge acquired by virtue of his appearance and toad-like noises on the bench). The lawyers of the respected Gonzales firm representing the chicken plant were confident.

On the day of trial, lo and behold: we had a visiting judge (the role of timing and luck in trials cannot be overstated). Granted, he was from Alabama but our client was not black and Alabama had few Hispanics at that time and virtually no history of discrimination against them. After hearing our first witness, the plaintiff himself, the judge called a recess and asked counsel to come into his chambers. Gathering the black robe about his ample body, he told us to go out and settle the case. He didn't ask us to try, he told us to do it.

My friends on the other side were dismayed and practically begging for mercy. Their client was adamant that he "didn't owe that Mes'cin a cent". I told them we would settle the case for half of what we pled for (not quite the same as we could prove as lost pay–the sole measure of damages then). It was a nice but not extravagant sum. Junior and I stood firm on this through a lot of hand wringing and that is what we settled for.

After that, those Gonzales lawyers seemed to think I was the fastest gun in the Western District of Texas and even associated me into, or referred me, cases in which they wanted a fast gun. For a brief, too brief, period of a few years, I entered the dark confines of Gonzales County like the Durango Kid. It was further proof that you could have fun in the practice of the law or that God loves a rummy.

For years, Junior called me on the anniversary date of the case. He once told me that the case had changed his life, made it possible for him to do things he never thought he could do like going into business for himself, which he successfully did. One case for one person can have bountiful results. I am not talking about money. Most of the employment discrimination clients cared far more about justice, vindication, than money.

Wounded Knee

Molly and I work away on the few legal cases remaining to me. In the old days, we called our bad cases "dog cases." In 2002, all my cases that are left (the big half dozen) are true dog cases because of my quadralegal. If I lose patience and start to explode–because the law and other lawyers can be so exasperating–I look to Molly who is always serene and easy and I relax a bit.

Looking back now, if I had to pinpoint the super cases of the 37 year run I've had in Austin as an essentially renegade radical lawyer, the first case I might think of is the defense of one of the participants in Wounded Knee II (the first Wounded Knee siege having occurred in 1890 when U.S. troops slaughtered 150 Lakota Ogala-Sioux men, women and children).

Wounded Knee II occurred in 1973 when a few hundred Indian activists and allies occupied the village at Wounded Knee on the Pine Ridge Reservation in South Dakota. After the 71-day siege ended with about 600 arrests, the U.S. Government charged almost two hundred defendants with various crimes. The National Lawyers Guild recruited attorneys from its membership, as did the larger more "mainstream" National Association of Criminal Defense Lawyers (NACDL).

Our firm was called by the Guild. I ventured to Sioux Falls, South Dakota in spring of 1974 for a meeting with legal defense committee people. My first contact was having lunch with three experienced and able defense lawyers: Joe Beeler and Al Krieger, both of New York, and Jim Shellow of Wisconsin. They had all become involved through the NACDL and were more criminal practitioners than interested in the politics of the clients so we were not establishing immediate rapport, as my law partner John Howard and I did later with Ken Tilsen, a senior lawyer who functioned as a sort of field general of the legal troops at Wounded Knee. Many of the trials in federal court, including ours, were moved to Lincoln, Nebraska.

Some of my recollections are fuzzy, as drinking and doping went on throughout the evening hours and sometimes in daytime depending upon whether it was a court day. I say it went on; we were sometimes involved, especially where beer was available. The legal defense committee, some defendants and some lawyers were housed at an abandoned Air Force base outside Lincoln through some agreement with local officials, as I recall. In retrospect our decision to bivouac there among the Movement troops was questionable.

At the time, John and I were both practicing alcoholics with a taste for just about any mind-altering substances. We were in trouble from the outset. We did our work, survived the minimalist and chaotic conditions of living at the barracks, not to mention the posturing, bickering and internecine politics. But the wear-and-tear on our bodies and psyches was debilitating, admittedly mostly from our own drinking and doping (far more drinking than doping, which was limited to marihuana and hashish).

After a few weeks, we won our case in no small part due to the reasonableness and fairness of a federal judge appointed by Richard Nixon, Warren Urbom. Our client had been charged with multiple counts including cattle rustling and assault on federal officers with a deadly weapon. It was the first and only time I have ever defended anyone for cattle rustling though I have practiced the entire 40 years in Texas.

Living amongst the defense committee people was like being in a perpetual political meeting. Movement people were the Olympic champions of meetings–too long, too full of rhetoric, too fractious, in short, too full of bullshit.

One tenet of the group was that everybody had to share the work of the barracks. So even if you had a heavy-duty court day ahead, you might find yourself expected to mop out the latrine the night before. And that is exactly what happened to us on the second night we were there. Down with elitism, up with egalitarianism, not to mention, even then, especially then, political correctness. In theory, it all sounded great. In reality, giant hassles arose when other duties, such as preparing for a critical evidentiary hearing, should clearly have taken precedence.

The nights were long, not hot for summer, the barracks uncomfortable. One night four guys from our barracks got arrested downtown and as the only lawyers not smart enough to make ourselves scarce, (not licensed in Nebraska, however) we were expected to go get the arrested persons out of jail. Our Wounded Knee client, who was called Hillbilly by all except the judge and prosecutor, climbed in the car and another fellow joined us. Off the four of us sailed into the night to bring justice to the plains.

We were arriving at the jail when I smelled a distinctive burning herbal odor emanating from the backseat. Hillbilly had fired up a major joint in our car. Not only that but soon the other guy with us had purloined a flashlight from a police cruiser parked next to us. I had visions of all of us being placed in jail with the clients. Somehow, we escaped that fate and even managed to get the clients out of jail in order for all of us to return to the all-night party at the barracks–but by order of the defense committee, outside of the barracks.

At 7 a.m. each morning, the crier came down the halls to every room to awaken us to another fun-filled day at Wounded Knee. Time to go forth and fight for the Movement. Coming to, reluctantly, I was soon advised that I had to be back in court with the four guys we had gotten out of jail the night before.

They were charged with the usual misdemeanors of rowdy boys–drunk and disorderly, criminal mischief–and the judge that morning made me practically turn over my birth certificate as surety for allowing them out of jail pending settings for trial. I made the necessary promises to the judge as an officer of the court (the one I was not licensed to practice in).

Months later they failed to appear and the judge up in Nebraska was ready to take me before the State Bar of Texas and would have except for a connection we had made in conversation that night of the arrests. A very good friend of the judge's who had worked in a big firm in D.C. with him was a guy from Abilene, of all places, I had known in high school and college debate, as well as UT law school. Plus, what could they get me for? I wasn't licensed in Nebraska and we had made full disclosure of that fact. I still felt badly about it. Other Guild lawyers advised thumbing my nose at the Nebraska people; militancy seemed to require it, but I tried to work it out and did.

Another wee hours conflagration between two guys over possession and the right to consume a single egg resulted in a shot being fired inside the barracks. My younger colleague John was awake but I was sleeping soundly, blissfully unaware that ordnance had gone off so nearby.

Years after we left the mid-west, Ken Tilsen told me that sometime during the siege of trials someone had committed suicide in the barracks. I could easily believe it. The barracks was a terrible place to stay during a tough trial. John's room was on the second floor of the barracks, mine was on the first. The rooms were no bigger than the jail cell we had seen downtown in Lincoln on the only occasion of our unlicensed practice of law in Nebraska. (Hillbilly's case was in federal court, where we were licensed.)

I have never liked the Midwest for reasons I probably couldn't and shouldn't articulate. Our several weeks in Lincoln had strongly reinforced that prejudice. On days we were not at the federal courthouse, I took to hanging out on the campus of the University of Nebraska.

I have always had an affinity for college campuses and I feel safe and comfortable there. I had spent essentially the better part of eight years of my life existing without visible means of support on campuses along I-35; I had gone to college and law school by hook or crook–scholarships, odd jobs from time to time, small contributions from family and mostly college loans. I felt I could survive on any major college campus unless it was in a dry town, booze not legal. So in Lincoln I sought the refuge of the big state university from the differing brands of chaos at the courthouse and the barracks.

But a lot of the time I felt like a stranger, coping with the legal task but not being in command, as I felt my idols would have been. Later, I learned from the best trial lawyer I have ever known, Warren Burnett, that most good trial lawyers did just what John and I were doing, right down to the drinking and winging it, partly because trials are unpredictable and you can't prepare for the unexpected.

Trials are simply war. On the battlefield, the best you can hope for is survival for your client and yourself amidst random deadly firefights. I could handle the court happenings by dint of a decade of experience; the out-of-court happenings were another thing entirely. I feel I was lucky to have the support of my fellow firm lawyer.

In fact, I had the able assistance of John on several important cases we tried and I thought highly of him as a person and a lawyer. At Wounded Knee, he was only two years out of law school. Throughout the entirety of his legal career of 16 years, he represented the little guy in righteous legal skirmishes, in the firm we both worked in and later as a sole practitioner in Austin. He was thorough and analytical, in many ways a born lawyer. He was funny and, in his way, eccentric–he stubbornly refused to stay at hotels where the sheets were not percale, but managed the conditions at the barracks.

One night as we sat outside feeling overworked, under-drunk, trying to stay a little sober to work, John looked up at a full moon and said, "We need some mood elevators." (It is ironic I guess that then we had no idea what anti-depressant drugs were, but we both wound up taking them). We bitched and moaned but we had fun with the legal work.

Working relationships undergo the greatest test in the crucible of such a case, and affection, even respect, can erode. We just strengthened a bond already well forged in prior work. It was a terrible blow and a great loss when John died in 1988 at only 41 years of age.

Our case like most of the Wounded Knee federal cases was a bench trial, judge only, no jury. So it proceeded in fits and starts according to the judge's convenience. I had the impression that, in effect, he was trying several cases at once. It was not of a piece, smoothly proceeding from start to finish, but rather an episodic series of surreal proceedings characterized by hangovers, barely controlled terror, happy surprises (and a couple not so happy).

People think of trials as being an orderly rational process involving confident, prepared and competent professionals. In your dreams and on television, maybe.

There was little order, only as much as Judge Urbom chose to impose. Even the time-honored symbolic practice of all standing when the judge entered the courtroom was defied and unenforced. The defendants and legal defense committee people refused to stand. To Judge Urbom's great credit (so unlike Judge Julius Hoffman in the Chicago 7 case and federal judges elsewhere) he ignored the violation of decorum and local court rules.

Sometimes sessions of court devolved into such general confusion there was just nothing to do but adjourn. Some proceedings even occurred in the judge's chambers, on and off the record. There were precious few dramatic moments, epiphanies, or brilliant courtroom stratagems. Stem-winding oratory was absent.

The real work was low-key, a process of all the principals jockeying, in a minefield of highly charged emotional bombs, in a very political case, to an understanding of what the patchwork confusion of evidentiary bits and pieces proved–or more tellingly, did not prove. Both sides sifting the evidence and highlighting what helped their own case.

In a sub-rosa way there was some rationality involved but it was seldom if ever apparent. I think that none of us–judge, prosecutors or John and I, certainly our client, who was habitually stoned out of his gourd–really knew what was happening when it was happening. As with so much of law practice, case management plays a primary role in reaching the desired result.

And in political cases often the outcome of the case is less important than having social issues exhibited for the larger society: making points overrides "winning". We felt our way along and, surprising to me, in the end the system worked, if by that we mean that our client was freed. In my view, the charges should have been dismissed, as they were. Most of the defendants at Wounded Knee II never should have been charged.

But I have to admit in a conventional legal sense our client might have been guilty of some narrow legal charges. He did participate in the taking of a cow for food. He did at times have a rifle which he may have pointed and fired at some point in the general direction of federal agents who were firing on the holed up Wounded Knee assemblage. They were garrisoned in the general store, as I recall, but when not being attacked by federal agents were doing little if any harm to anyone.

Fortunately, justice was served by the inability of the U.S. Attorney's office to prove the charges, which they are required to do beyond a reasonable doubt. We strove for our client's freedom, not for the defense lawyer's ego boost of getting him off, but because he had been a participant in an important, even historic social protest on behalf of one of the groups of victims of America's homegrown holocausts. What we did to American

Indians was genocidal and something we don't talk about or make any meaningful restitution for. It is, along with slavery of African Americans, the darkest shame we carry.

On the day Nixon resigned as president, a group of us was on our way out of Lincoln, free from the spooky legal proceedings and the insanity that pervaded the barracks. Our client was free of charges he had been under for nearly a year and for which he could have served a long sentence in federal prison.

It had been nothing like what I pictured in my imagination before driving to Lincoln. All I wanted on that August day in 1974 was to be free from the madness we had lived in for weeks.

Yet, over time I would come to look upon this crazy experience as one of the most important trials of my time as a lawyer, one of the greatest victories for the people (as we called such triumphs). By any standard, it seems significant legal work, forever etched in history, even if the doing of it had seemed less than a Technicolor epic of courtroom drama. For years now, certainly during the dreadful '90s, I have cherished this experience as evidence that validates my effort and intent of all these years I have endeavored to be a Movement lawyer. I came away with a strong respect and sense of solidarity with the American Indian Movement and Indian people.

The opportunity to contribute where it mattered a lot came at a bad time; we were less than heroic in our carrying out of the mission we had. Booze made us slip and slide on the stage of the historical trials of Wounded Knee defendants, but our stumbling was outside the courtroom. It did not really occur to me then that it was to be one of the zeniths of my life in the law.

It was like earning our spurs, undergoing the experience that would buttress us in our future trials. To us it was the space shuttle that indicated we had the right stuff. In the end, we prevailed.

The way lawyers are wont to keep score, victory is what matters. However, we had always known better. Of far, far more importance, we were there putting our legal skills and credentials to the service of the Movement in America at a time and place that were unique and very meaningful. Nothing will ever change that. I've always felt that I cherished the experience even though it was rough. But maybe it is because it was rough. Wounded Knee II was one of the most significant legal battles of the Movement in the 20th century.

From Law Commune to Law Firm–Still Slackers?

My quadralegal, Molly, reminds me that it is the rip-roaring, volatile, often highly stressful times that I tend to recall so well. Times before Molly's time.

I first was hospitalized for depression itself in summer of 1975. At that time, Pooh was living with her mom in Blanco, a hill country town, 50 miles from Austin. My mother had taken a sharp downturn in her condition. Life became a burden almost unbearable. Anyone who suffers from depression understands well what I mean.

I left Shoal Creek Hospital after a very short stay. Soon I learned that Pooh was coming to live with Nancy and me in August. She would go to an Austin junior high in the fall. It meant I would have to get up no later than 6:30 a.m., fix her breakfast and get her to the school bus stop. Since my divorce in 1972 I had never had this primary responsibility for her and the prospect of it scared me. But mostly it was a thrilling and wonderful thing to think my daughter would be living with us.

It was the best therapy I could have gotten. I loved every moment of the years she lived with us until graduating high school and beyond, through her first semester at the University of Texas.

There was a very special bond between us and at that time, I was surer of it than any other human connection in my life. After college when she lived in New Mexico for a couple of years, Ellie cried as she had to board her plane back to New Mexico and after it took off I cried, too.

In 1976 Steve Russell and I took up the case of a Hispanic woman in a rural area far northeast of Austin who had been seriously injured in a car accident which was clearly caused by the other driver's negligence. She had consulted an influential Anglo lawyer in the area. He had stalled her, done nothing and never advised her of the statute of limitations which shortly ran out, barring her from suing the driver at fault. She went to the ACLU and they got us to take the case (not an uncommon experience). We sued the lawyer for legal malpractice (a type of suit I handled on sundry occasions).

When we went into this tiny, incredibly insular area in a county with a reputation for racism, it was like going back in time–way back. Steve and I appeared for a jury trial to find that virtually every other lawyer in a three-county area was there, one way or another, to defend and support the defendant lawyer. To say they were confident of victory is to refine the art of understatement. Our client testified in Spanish through an interpreter, the defendant lawyer was influential and supported by many other prominent lawyers and we were carpetbag lawyers from Austin! Which way would anyone bet this would turn out?

Regardless of the factors against us, there was a core of independent and strong jurors. We won a huge victory by putting several women who were married to doctors and other well-respected local citizens on the jury. It was a gamble. Naturally, the local lawyers expected these women to be for them.

The jury argued for hours as the judge, the defendant and the tri-county bar membership, and Steve and I could hear them in the old, small county courthouse. We could not hear what they were saying, only the voices raised in anger. The hubbub went on for hours before the women prevailed over the good old boys and gave us our verdict.

On this occasion cynicism vanished as we savored justice truly done. And we got out of the county fast as we could before a posse formed.

After the old firm broke up in 1977, Brady and I had taken a year off, meaning we had no office and did a modicum of legal work. Our standing daily rendezvous at the Chili Parlor, a bar near the capitol (one of the very few Austin places I have written about that is still there), was around 4 p.m., to talk about what we could do with the rest of our lives besides be lawyers.

In late summer of that year, we both got involved in representing a bunch of our colleagues at the bar in a suit against the State Bar of Texas, which had just imposed a mandatory assessment on all lawyers to pay for an $8 million dollar boondoggle: the new Texas Law Center, which the Bar sold to lawyers as being paid for by voluntary contributions, and then reneged on that. A lot of Texas lawyers, the ones not in the big firms of the rug lawyers catered to by the Bar, were hopping mad.

When we tried the case in federal court, Warren Burnett and Laird Palmer, noted Texas lawyers, were in the unaccustomed role of being named plaintiffs and star witnesses on our side. After an all too brief trial in federal court, we lost.

When Warren was ready to go back to Odessa, Brady and I gave him a ride to the airport by way of the bar at the Driskill Hotel, where he had several drinks with hard liquor (ethanol as he would say) and a stop for beer. He bought a couple of six-packs. When we got out to the airport it turned out he was not taking a commercial flight but directed us to the airpark for small private aircraft where Warren then loaded his pockets down with the cans of beer. With horror we realized he was about to get in his own plane and fly back to his office in Odessa.

The visions Brady and I had conjured up at the Chili Parlor, of newspapers we would found (the Buda Bugle) or the bar we would open, would dissipate as we began to face our destiny. Law practice. We found a great old house (built in 1915) in central Austin on Blanco Street that was being remodeled. We bought it late in 1978, in time to get it finished to order for a law office.

Much about the old firm had been good but there were many personality clashes and outright fights internally and by the end the term "firm meeting" struck fear and dread in all our hearts. The new firm was just Brady Coleman and me and we got along well. Most of the time the prevailing aura around the office was easy going. In terms of legal productivity–I'm not just talking about money either–and pure contentment with the practice, it was the best time of all.

We had been partners for nearly ten years when we garnered our assets together to buy the old house at 617 Blanco Street for our law office.

I did not suspect it at the time but our years on Blanco Street were probably the happiest ones of my legal "career" (a word I abhor). My capability as a lawyer was maxed out through this time culminating with the jury trial victory in the Jack Ruby gun case, litigation over the historic .38 caliber gun that killed Lee Harvey Oswald.

There had really been two themes in the old firm, or commune, which came to be the law firms Simons, Cunningham & Coleman; and later Simons, Cunningham, Coleman, Nelson & Howard; and briefly Simons, Cunningham, Coleman, Nelson, Howard & Schieffelin. Most prominent was our political mission and identity.

But secondly we had embodied a slacker ethos that has now come to be so associated with Austin. (Richard Linklater's movie "Slacker", about Austin, came out in 1991.) Looking back I attribute a lot of this to Brady and myself. I think we both felt, having practiced in conventional settings, that we wanted our office to be fundamentally different in everyday life as well as concept. All our offices were in large old houses, near the Travis County courthouse.

Early on we abandoned the coat and tie except for courtroom appearances and adopted extreme informality among the lawyers, clerks, legal workers and hangers-on who hung around. On occasion, joints were torched in the office.

At one time a ne'er-do-well fellow essentially lived in our office, often taking calls in the wee hours for one of us from some distressed or jailed client, before he borrowed money from us and disappeared forever. An ancient craggy black man probably lived in the backyard or even under the building. He would cut the grass in front of the building, or say he did, now and then for cash. We knew him only as old Cal.

Inconspicuous consumption ruled the day. You had to have a shapeless corduroy jacket and some unpolished, scuffed boots to wear to court, never a Brooks Brothers suit and Lucchese cowboy boots of exotic leathers as favored by our colleagues at the courthouse. Most of us had battered VW bugs in contrast to the Travis County lawyer car of choice, the Mercedes-Benz. My VW had once had a sun roof but it had blown completely off on my way back hung over from a trip to Houston. I hadn't bothered looking for it.

Nancy had taken to covering the hole in the roof with bright floral contact paper, making that car quite a sight. Ellie asked me to let her out a block from O. Henry Junior High when I took her to school. A client had once followed me from my office to Municipal Court where, as usual, we waited. At last he got a funny expression on his face and finally blurted out, "Man, you a beeg lawyer, why you drive a piece of shit like that?" I explained to him it was a classic.

No one in our group had ever heard, much less used the term "billable hours," and all who worked there got an equal say about what work we did and how the place was run. Pomposity was a sin not easily forgiven (but occasionally practiced). We partied together and played soft ball games with utter disregard of the rules–the very way we ran the office. Ambition, drudgery and rectitude were eschewed by all. The number one requirement for the practice of the law (outside of our political aim) was that it be fun.

It was not uncommon of an afternoon to hear one of the lawyers bellow out "Jeremiah was a bullfrog" or a clutch of folks breaking into the stirring rendition of "Oh Lord, Won't You Buy Me A Mercedes-Benz", a song we always got around to at parties, or Kristofferson's other classics, "Help Me Make It Through the Night" or "Me and Bobby McGee". The music of our happy times together, when I hear it now, reminds me that through it all we loved each other.

Once we all gathered in one of the lawyer offices and watched an amateur porn video that a client made and for which he encountered legal trouble. Shortly afterwards a legal worker and one of the lawyers left the office together in mid-afternoon. We regularly had parties in our office where the usual suspects came: the writers of the Rag, an underground newspaper; people from Greenbriar, the alternative free-school; Satva, a vegetarian communal eatery on the Drag at UT; Oat Willie's, a head shop; and of course, the artists, slackers, dope dealers and alcoholics from the venerable and cavernous Armadillo World Headquarters, a bar, music venue, gathering spot to eat, drink and celebrate the coming Revolution. Over the years, there were many other counter-culture, alternative institutions, usually communal, always slacker. These places were public features of the community we were part of.

In the partnership that Brady and I had in the '80s after the firm dissolved, the slacker aspect was alive and well even during a decade we dubbed "The Real Estate Years". Brady regularly appeared in the office in cut-offs and tee-shirts with his large, one-eyed dog, Zeke. He became put out with me when, post-sobriety, I started to act more like a lawyer. He gently disparaged my sometime wearing of "real suits and ties" and made it clear that any attention to keeping regular hours was out of place. Of course, he was right. We spoke harshly to each other almost never and I still have no better friend than Brady.

We won a surprising number of cases but of the ones we lost, the hardest to take was a death penalty case. We did not try the case but Brady and I came into it at the behest of the ACLU (by way of the incomparable Dorothy Browne) in the post-conviction, post-appeals stage. In other words, at the last gasp desperation stage. It was back at a time when executions in Texas were carried out at midnight, a fitting time for such a barbaric practice.

I can still remember the agony of sweating out a last minute stay request at the Court of Criminal Appeals, the highest court for criminal cases in Texas. And the heartbreak of having it denied on a 5-4 split vote (one of the votes to stop the executioner was my old friend Judge Sam Houston Clinton). I had never met the client. Nevertheless, his execution hit hard. It certainly wasn't the only lost case I have shed tears over. There is so much–life itself–riding on a capital case that to lose is to fail to prevent a murder, albeit by the State.

In my opinion, no lawyers in the United States are doing more important and meaningful legal work than the gallant cadre of attorneys that regularly fight the death penalty, case by case. I have immense respect for them.

Sobriety

Molly gets a funny look in her poodle's visage when I talk of being a drunk. She came into our home in Clarksville when we were several years sober—she has only known us in sobriety.

The hard-drinking trial lawyer is a cliché. The reality of it is a day-to-day nightmare. Alcohol is the perfect drug for a trial lawyer. At day's end in a trial, one is both drained of all energy and wound up tight. Alcohol addresses both conditions. It relaxes you and simultaneously gives you energy. It is the answer. Until tomorrow morning when you wake up and face another day feeling like shit. Alcohol is the trial lawyer's perfect drug also because it holds his destruction in its smooth, soothing liquid. Many trial lawyers are self-destructive, certainly egotistical, self-dramatizing. So the elixir offers us a smooth descent into the nether regions away from responsibility—something which we avidly seek and try to escape.

When I drank I did some things sexually which are outside the bounds of conventional behavior. In fact, I recognized few boundaries when it came to consenting adults, particularly up until Nancy returned to Austin on that glorious fall day in 1972. That changed my life dramatically; so did the miracle of sobriety in the summer of 1980.

By the time I checked into St. David's Hospital in the early morning hours of July 24, 1980, I had had all the booze I could ever drink and stay alive.

The losses were phenomenal. I lost a wife, a son, and I lost Nancy from 1964 to 1972 and nearly lost her forever toward the end of my life as a drunk. And I had lost all hope by that summer morning in July 1980. I was simply fighting for my life. My mother had always said: survive now, figure out why later.

I was operating on that philosophy and nothing more except my love for my daughter. I did not want to leave her fatherless even though at that time she was 17 years old. It was virtually the only significant relationship in my life that was intact. It was not the first time that I thought of her and resolved to survive in the midst of a dark despond. Many times over my adult drinking career, and after Ellie was born, I caught hold and refused to go under by thinking of her.

By the summer of 1980 my drinking was a grim daily necessity. In March, I had gotten sick before, during and after a federal civil trial. At that time, I was diagnosed with pancreatitis. I stayed dry for a few days, but at the wedding of my former law partner, John Howard, and my old friend Carole Jones, I scarfed champagne (again that bubbly form of the elixir). I was off to the races for several more months until I fell from the cumulative weight of the addiction, from chronic despair and terror, and from the pain in my gut caused by the afflicted pancreas. I was awake all night, bouncing off the walls. The booze I had on that last day was still in my system. It had all come to a head for me.

I was admitted at 7 a.m. to St. David's Hospital with the graciously given help of my friend and ex-wife, Helen, where I remained for a few days, drying out, ruminating glumly on life without the elixir–and I feared, without Nancy. I imagined that we could not have fun without drink. Sure, look how much fun we had been having! Constant quarrels, when we were even talking to each other, recriminations, suspicions, threats to move out. What fun.

I was sure she would regard me as a drag, a party-pooper, and she would want to go merrily on her way. It scared me worse than the unthinkable idea of never drinking again. The truth was that we were headed toward a break-up; we were about to lose each other. We had fought all the time we drank which was all the time.

Neither of us knew that the best was yet to come for us, a new life filled with new, fully realized sensations and a mutual compact of love and commitment such as we had never had before. Our relationship matured in sobriety as it never would have otherwise.

Three days out of the hospital, I was ready for a drink, at wit's end, writhing in psychic discomfort, desperate for something, mostly for a drink. I made one of the best calls I've ever made in my life. For help. I called Dr. John Boston, a shrink I had been seeing, who finally saw I was alcoholic, powerless over alcohol.

He asked me if I would see an AA member if one came to me at my house. I was frantic. I said oh, OK. The doctor called a recovering alcoholic priest who in turn called a fellow named Mac McKemie, an illustrious and completely fantastic 51-year-old alky with 9 years sobriety in AA. In short order, Mac pulled his long Cadillac sedan into my short driveway. He was a big tall guy and plain spoken. He wanted to take me to the Suburban Club AA: just drive me out there right then, in midafternoon.

I expressed concern (as I've heard other sufferers do so many times since) about whether it was somehow religious, something about God in their slogans, that "big book." His words were inspired. Mac said: "to hell with that Goddamned fucking shit. Do you want to not have to take a drink?" I said I wanted not to have to take a drink. I knew only too well exactly where a single drink would lead. Mac said: "Well then, let's just go out there."

We boarded the dreadnought Caddy and went out to Suburban. No meetings were scheduled at that time of day but there were a handful of people around and Mac corralled them into a kind of impromptu meeting just for me. As long as I live, I won't forget those amazing, wonderful people, who that day obviously cared about me enough to talk to me, convey concern and love in a way I think only alcoholics can do toward each other.

That day a doctor with five years sobriety told me God as referred to in the 12 Steps could be anything. He said: God can be this cup right here, anything, whatever you want it to be. A higher power. At that point in time the cup was probably a higher power than me; I had hit bottom. In AA, coffee was consumed by the gallon so cups were all around and seemed as good a higher power as any.

In a few minutes, surrounded by the love of half a dozen other alcoholics, taking their time with me, talking from the heart, saying nothing profound–just talking "the program"–I lost my desperate need for the elixir. For the rest of that day, I had not the need for a cold beer or a whiskey. I thought: so that was it: one day at a time. The only day that counted was today and one should do whatever it took not to have to take a drink.

There would be other days I needed help, I needed the fellowship of other drunks, or I needed to read their words in the Big Book. All of that has always been there. Sometimes I sustained my own sobriety by being there for some other newly arrived, desperate drunk, helping him or her not to have to take that drink.

Sure, it all sounds trite, simplistic, too easy. But it works and that is all I need to know. I got my life back from sickness, fear and oblivion. It has been a miracle for me. I do not need to feel intellectually superior. It just keeps me sober to accept it for what it is. I am still not religious.

Maybe I should be. Because to my astonishment, Nancy joined me in sobriety, finding meaning for herself in the "simple" program of AA. Not only did we not lose each other, we found each other all over again, better than ever before. This time we missed nothing from being too impaired to recall it or too anesthetized to appreciate or too dull to even see what the moment or year was, how magnificent or poignant. Life itself was returned to us.

In that summer of 1980, we suddenly seemed to have time we never had before. Instead of sitting zombie-like before the TV, drinks in hand, whacking our senses, we sat on our front porch swing, aware now of the magic of summer nights, sights, sounds, smells. We actually talked to each other. Our senses became keen again. We walked the half mile to the

Clarksville Cream Shop every night to get ice cream. I loved ice cream as a boy; I had hardly had any at all in the last 20 years of drinking.

I read everything I could get on the history of AA. I was deeply fascinated, as my sponsor Mac had been, by the history of the fellowship. When I occasionally hit rough waters, I called Mac.

Once, very early in our sobriety, Nancy and I came upon one of those Saturday afternoons when we were at loose ends. The urge to buy a 6-pack was strong. I called Mac who had us immediately come out to his house at Lake Travis. He and his wife Carolyn made us feel right at home, fixed sandwiches for us, talked to us, showed us the beauty of the lake. The urge to buy a 6-pack or a fifth disappeared with the setting sun.

That day Mac told us if we needed to we could stay there–live there!–for awhile. Needless to say, we would never have taken advantage or imposed on them to that extent. But it showed me how total was this good man's commitment to help me stay sober, how giving and generous was his love for fellow alcoholics. It moved us very much, the more so because it was quietly and clearly genuine to the core.

Mac never engaged in posturing. What he said today, he meant tomorrow. I was blessed to have him as a sponsor; I was blessed to have known him. (He died in the mid-'90s.)

Yet, Mac and I were as different as two men could be. He was a Republican, a conservative businessman, old and rich, Catholic by registration. I was none of those things, quite the contrary. But we were brought together because of a disease (according to the American Medical Association) we both had, by the depths of depravity and craving we both knew so well and by a spirituality we both found that had absolutely nothing to do with being Catholic or Protestant or agnostic.

I read somewhere that Aldous Huxley (not alcoholic) came to regard AA as a phenomenal social institution, unique in its egalitarianism, tolerance and lack of structure. How else would Mac McKemie and I ever have looked into each other's eyes and found a bond that transcended the external, phony constructs of our society? It is almost worth the pain of many, many nights (and mornings) battling the demons of alcoholism, to have known some of the fine people I have known in AA.

When I called Mac to have a chat, he inevitably asked me to meet him at the posh Headliners Club on top of a downtown bank building for lunch. So for years I thought the way to stay sober was to go to the Headliners Club for a steak. He was simply one of the finest human beings I've ever known in my life and I loved him. (I learned in both the Movement and AA that it is okay to say you love people.) AA has been one of the greatest learning experiences of my life besides being the thing that saved my ass.

Later, in that most peculiar decade of our time, the '80s, Alcoholics Anonymous became a mainstream, "in" place to go and be seen. The only requirement for membership is a desire to stop drinking and/or drugging. No one is turned away. In its fashionableness, AA lost some of its unique character for a time. But the basic principles are so sound that it has endured this period.

Perhaps the challenge now is the recent pervasive religiosity asserted by the aggressively "Christian" fundamentalists or those who blindly follow them. They don't own AA which is NOT a religious group and never should be.

In August of 1980, with a month of sobriety, my dear old friend, surrogate father, political and lawyerly guru Maury Maverick invited Nancy and me to spend a weekend at his "country place," a small, comfortable house on the Medina River in the town of Castroville. I had actually asked for an audience because I knew Maury had quit drinking some years earlier. I was looking for his help and, as always, it was magnanimously extended. Maury knew something about drinking. He told me he had gotten two bits of advice about drinking. His stepfather the historian Walter Prescott Webb had told him: when you drink, sip a glass of good bourbon over an evening of good conversation. His father, the colorful Maury Maverick, Sr. had told him: when you drink, drink a fifth of whiskey as fast as you can and get into a fistfight over the Catholic Church. Both Maury Junior and I had followed the latter advice.

Our time on the Medina with a hurricane hitting the Gulf Coast a couple hundred miles away was helpful. Maury himself only came out for awhile on Saturday afternoon when I talked with him about my "decision" to stop drinking (and keep on living). In his gruff, low-key way he gave me the faith that it was possible to overcome having been a drunk.

By early 1981, with 6 months sobriety, I was feeling both the elation of being sober (though the true "pink cloud" period started later and lasted for almost the whole balance of the '80s) and the strain of dealing with the world without any chemical help, without my old best friend alcohol. My mother died after over a decade of deteriorating and the last of those years living in a vegetative state. In her last month of life, I was involved with a big time federal criminal case heading toward jury trial. What made it worse was a client who had been a friend and whose view of the situation, the law and the criminal justice system was badly askew. The case got tried and the huge strain of it passed (though I was somewhat crushed but not at all surprised by his conviction).

The Black Dog

Molly says Winston Churchill spoke of the "black dog of depression" and, as a black dog, she takes exception to that. Settling nearby, she sleeps (at work) and I wonder what she is dreaming about.

Depression nearly killed me several times, including the papa bear of my episodes of depression, which occurred after the start of sobriety. It came on relentlessly over a period of months. Depression builds up, grinds you down, until it takes hold and it is itself the dominant reality of your life.

Mine usually went away after a week or two. I was first hospitalized for it in 1975. After two days, I considered the psych ward of the hospital worse than the cloud of depression I couldn't seem to escape. I think I took some kind of tricyclic antidepressant, such as Elavil or Tofranil, at that time and freaked out a little at some very slight side effects. Then, I briefly took lithium, the only effect of which was gastrointestinal distress. The initial side effects would have passed most likely but I gave up or got fearful and stopped these medications.

Depression usually hit me in summer although I was fairly depressed regularly around Christmas. For years, my self-medication was alcohol. Which is a depressant itself and contraindicated; usually it made my depression worse.

But if the binges were the descent into hell, the sobering up, after a certain point, was a ray of sunshine. Just stopping the intake of booze, enduring the withdrawal and reaching a clearing lifted my spirits. For years, this was the process of dealing with my depression: drinking, getting worse, enduring withdrawal from alcohol for the little ray of sunshine at the end.

Both of my parents suffered from depression. You could say it killed my dad. At least one doctor thought my mother's organic brain syndrome was caused by shock treatments she got in the early `70s. Certainly in the long run alcohol greatly exacerbated my depression. They went hand-in-hand.

On the criminal docket, aside from one or two murder cases, which were nevertheless not complicated, the hairiest case I had came, as luck would have it, in the first year of my sobriety when the AA sponsors tell you not to do anything too stressful. An old client of mine was a tax preparer who had discovered a foolproof method for obtaining fat refunds for his clients. He therefore had many clients who came in droves from towns across the state so this tax wizard could work his wonders that brought the big refund checks from the IRS. The IRS had long been after him.

In late 1980 he was finally indicted on 42 counts of tax fraud in federal court. The case was set for trial by jury only a couple of weeks after my mother died in March 1981. It was the most complex criminal case I ever had, with the additional problem of a client badly out of touch with reality.

The day we selected a jury, March 31, 1981, President Reagan and Jim Brady were shot by John Hinckley. As though this momentous event (evoking the horrors of the assassinations of the '60s) had triggered it, I fell prey to a great anxiety. Being nervous before trials was a common experience; it was natural and necessary. But this was different.

That night after I realized what I was facing with essentially no help, I cratered from the anxiety and a sense of inadequacy. I immediately contacted one of my AA sponsors and had a meeting with him at the Suburban Club. The following morning I went directly to the office of his accounting firm and together we telephoned the judge and told him that I was being hospitalized at Shoal Creek Hospital, psychiatric ward. This was true enough. I had called my old shrink John Boston, who had a hand in getting me into AA, and simply told him I was freaking out over this big case. I don't think at that time there was any other diagnosis. He was happy to order the hospitalization to bail me out of the immediate crisis. That day when my law partner Brady Coleman appeared in court, the case was re-set until April 21st, giving me time to find an answer. The hospitalization ended when federal Judge William Sessions gave this three-week delay.

Rushing from my hospital room to my office, I called Warren Burnett, an old friend and (need I say it again?), the best trial lawyer I have ever known. Warren practiced all over Texas out of the West Texas town of Odessa. He was in great demand and hard to find or get through to on the phone.

In 1978 a group of lawyers angry over a "special assessment" the State Bar was imposing on all Texas lawyers sued the Bar. I handled the case, the second time I had sued the Texas licensing authority (a third opportunity to break the tie in outcomes has not appeared). Warren had been a named plaintiff in that suit and at the trial he was a star witness.

Typically, he had not hesitated to allow his name and estimable reputation to be used in controversial litigation to challenge the legal establishment. After first meeting at the wild Wimberley Conference, we had become better acquainted in working on a case against 21 local activists arrested at the Chuckwagon, a student snack bar and lounge area in the Texas Union at UT. The DA had taken a very hard-line tack and gotten felony indictments on some cockamamie conspiracy to riot theory. None of the cases stuck as Cam and I were joined by Sam Houston Clinton, David Richards and Warren Burnett in the defense of the Chuck Wagon 21.

A few years later I worked closer with Burnett on the lawsuit against the State Bar. Probably because of that I was able to get him on the line that spring of 1981. I know he knew I had problems with the case, or problems in general, and he roundly sympathized with a lawyer who could not partake. To my great relief, he agreed to become co-counsel in the upcoming criminal jury trial in federal court and arranged to come forthwith to Austin.

There was a large fee on the table (tax preparation for scads of clients had made my client wealthy). But it was not that which induced him to take on this difficult case so late in the game. Because the first thing he did was to insist on giving me half of the fee, which was entirely his, had he chosen to take it. Money meant little to Burnett. He had made plenty of it. He was simply one of the most generous and big-hearted lawyers it was ever my pleasure to know.

In addition, he had a rapier wry wit and willingness to slay dragons. He did not shy away from the hard cases. Working with him was good fun.

Burnett's help and encouragement of younger lawyers was legendary. He got into the case and gave me half of his fee because he wanted to help me and I will never forget it. I would have done anything for him.

After Warren entered the case with me, he picked my brain for three weeks as he "got the case" from me and the clients verbally. I don't think he ever read any of the voluminous discovery or pleadings. He didn't have to; I knew the case cold since I had lived with it for a few years as the IRS sought to get the goods on the client.

The way he wanted to work was to get a six-pack and drive around (I drove) while we talked about the details of the case. One warm spring afternoon as we set out on this unorthodox manner of trial preparation, he directed me to pull into a convenience store for the purpose of buying beer. I said no, there's a better place down the street. Whereupon he looked at me like I was nuts, and said: "Better? The only way it could be better, would be for it to be closer." That's also an indication of how incredibly analytical his mind was–by instinct.

The three weeks we worked on the case was some of the best time I ever spent preparing for trial, usually drudgery. We tried the case in April for almost two weeks, in the court of Judge William Sessions, who was not one of Warren's favorite federal judges, it was clear. (I have to say that Judge Sessions treated me with great courtesy and consideration–probably because he never before had a lawyer carried off to the loony bin right after jury selection.)

Warren seemed optimistic after his eloquent final argument and the strident, screeching one of the prosecutor. But the jury returned, after deliberating a day and a half, with a verdict of guilty on all 42 counts in the indictment. It was over except for the appeal. The client was going to prison, which was a crushing blow to all of us although I had realized it was an unwinnable case.

The U.S. Attorney had threatened the defendant's tax clients with prosecution unless they testified against him and there were many witnesses who did just that to save their own butts. We could not condemn them too much for running scared; they were all just working folks. Warren had quarterbacked a spirited and, I thought, effective defense. We had been caught up in an impassioned advocacy for our client but we had some fun along the way.

I had managed to stay sober, as I ground toward the first anniversary of my new life. Warren had quizzed me over the 5 weeks we prepared for and tried the case about the fact that I had a condition which ruled out "the taking of ethanol", which he clearly regarded as a sad pass for anyone, but especially a trial lawyer, who had a special dispensation for the solace of drink. He had even found time to do some research on pancreatitis in the fervent hope it would never afflict him.

In a habeas corpus petition hearing years after the trial, the client, desperate to get out of prison, had asserted ineffective assistance of counsel as grounds for re-trial. To buttress this ridiculous argument, he claimed Warren was drunk while trying the case. (Most people who knew Warren might believe he was drunk but not that he was ineffective.) Appearing as a witness in the hearing, Burnett as much as said he was drunk during the trial. He was still trying to help the client.

I was there at the trial day after day in close quarters with him at counsel table and there is no doubt that he never even had a drink during the hours of trial. As a recent former drunk myself, I could tell if he had although I was not asked about it when I testified. The writ was denied.

My first jury trial back in the day had been against Racehorse Haynes in night court in Pasadena. And since then I have seen many trial lawyers. Warren Burnett was pure and simple the best.

As summer set in that first year of sobriety, the old familiar darkness descended. The disease of depression, which I had medicated for over 20 years with the elixir, was upon me with a vengeance. It got worse and worse. In July I went into Shoal Creek for real.

I wasn't just freaked out over a case, I was clinically depressed. Dr. Dick Alexander, my expert witness in the Roky Erickson case a few years earlier, was now my psychiatrist. I was deep in the pit for weeks. I still believe I grieved for the loss of my old best friend, indeed my deity, none other than the elixir. Like so many other alcoholics I have known, the bottom fell out for me then.

I believed I was having attacks of pancreatitis and I could have been but not from drinking. So my family doctor gave me a supply of Demerol for the pain which I took for awhile. It did nothing but possibly make things worse. I had wanted the pain to be physical (and therefore treatable) but that was not all it was.

I was in and out of the hospital, once in the suicide prevention unit though I was not suicidal in my own mind. This was the deepest, longest and, so far, the last bout of depression I have ever had. I commenced taking Pamelor (or nortriptyline,) a tricyclic antidepressant, at that time and I still have to take it, which I am glad to do to prevent any future attacks. No one apparently knows exactly why this class of drugs works to prevent depression in millions of people. But it does not work for some people.

My one time law partner John Howard was taking a similar anti-depressant but still suffering severe depression when he died suddenly of heart problems in July 1988. It is time to stop acting like there's anything wrong with taking medication for depression or any other medical problem. Depression is a physical illness just like diabetes is.

I am only thankful that there is a medication that keeps my depression in check, allows me to live a normal life free from those pits of despair. I probably will have to take the medication the rest of my life and that is no big deal. Whatever the expense, it's a life saving med, worth it at any price.

I have lived to see my 60th birthday and considerably beyond because of the gift of grace, sobriety, and because of medication. Without both of these I have no doubt I would not be alive to watch my four beautiful grandsons grow up to be boys and men.

The minority of AA people who cluck righteously about taking any "mind altering drugs" are woefully misguided when they include anti-depressants or other drugs that effectively control mental disorders, which stem from physical causes. Anti-depressants work slowly over time to increase the presence of serotonin or other neurotransmitters in the brain to stop and prevent the capture of the mind by sadness, hopelessness and anhedonia. Lives are literally saved by these medications.

With each study and disclosure it is clearer that many people suffer from the malady of depression. It is not a character flaw or weakness. Sufferers can't "snap out of it" or "buck up and keep a stiff upper lip" and all the nonsensical shibboleths we grew up hearing. Conversely, the absence of depression is not a sign of strong character any more than not having diabetes or Lou Gehrig's disease is. Depression is a medical problem requiring a medical solution and fortunately pharmaceuticals are the most effective treatment and can frequently alleviate and prevent the debilitating disease that kills.

That summer 1981, I was barely coping. I was extremely upset to be going downhill even though I was sober. The episode started rather dramatically on a Saturday in July.

Around 5 p.m. a sudden on-set of panic, a strong sense of a chasm in my mood, almost a feeling of falling. In the bathroom pantry all I had to take was Valium, before Xanax, the universal household tranquilizer. It did nothing.

Slowly over the next few days, darkness descended until I was enveloped in it. Everything seemed hopeless; there was no happy aspect to anything I thought of. The emptiness was all-consuming and I wanted to do nothing day after day. My old friend and good psychiatrist, Dick Alexander, put me in Shoal Creek Hospital on two different occasions, the second time on the suicide prevention ward. I had plummeted to the bottom of my pit.

It was, I am still convinced, grief over the loss of my mother, who had played a major role in my life, and my best friend, the go-to guy, alcohol. Life without the elixir was at times unspeakably hard for that first year. I have known a lot of recovering drunks who experienced that pit of despair in the first year of sobriety. Mac described his depression in the first year of his sobriety as "the bottom fell out." Since then, as a sponsor of others in AA, I've heard this many times.

I never consciously thought of suicide. It was not an option for me. I knew what it did to those left behind. I had too much of my mother's spunky will to live, never-say-die spirit. There was self-pity, remorse over every petty little misdeed of 42 years of living, anhedonia. I withdrew into dark daily solitude at home (when I was not in the hospital). I've never before or since experienced such total despair although there was worse terror in the one time I had delirium tremens from drinking.

I was determined to live through it. Somewhere in the back of my despondent mind I knew it would pass and that I had to endure. The routine at Shoal Creek was tough for one deep in depression. Up at 7 a.m. for breakfast. Although I ate almost nothing at all for a month and my weight dropped to 126 pounds on a 6'1" frame. I did manage to eat a bowl of ice cream each night that Nancy religiously brought to me. Aside from that, I got down virtually no food.

This was the first time (of many) Nancy proved what a loyal, loving and tenacious ally she is. She came twice a day every single day. She sat with me in the grim half light of my room or, worse, in the ersatz cheer of the over lighted day room with other zombies scattered about. She never had to say "I'm with you; you have my full unending support." She showed me by her steadfast daily deeds. By her presence, by everything she did. I cannot remember through the fog all the little things she constantly did to reassure me, give me a sense of hope, stay the course as my main ally in this world. I don't know if I would have made it without her.

Six months earlier we had been on the brink in the alcoholic daily rows of our disputatious existence of breaking up for good. I know it would have happened had we continued drinking.

There is a theory that the chief way each fellow survives is by strategic alliances–with a spouse, lover, parent, business partner. Strategic alliances get you through the pitfall-laden world. I have had such alliances with my mother, friends at school, debate partners, Helen, my daughter, my law partner, Brady. Most of all with Nancy; she has never let me down. Some strategic alliances last a year, or five years, some throughout life. I have been fortunate in the strategic alliance department.

During the despair of 1981, I remember thinking that I would be OK if I could hang on until the annual AA weekend gathering at Brownwood, Texas–the Lakeside Conference in September. We had first gone to this joyous gathering in the previous year, our first year of sobriety. It had shown us that there were people who were genuinely happy about being sober, whereas we had thought it was a long dark tunnel to trudge. We really first saw sober joy in Brownwood.

The worst of the depression broke up like an oceanic ice block in spring in the latter part of August. Coincidentally, it was around the time Nancy's father died after a yearlong battle with cancer. I had to drive several hundred miles to be with her at the funeral in Wichita Falls. In the space of six months we had each had a parent die. I was weak from hospitalization and psychotropic drugs, but I was able to drive the distance in one day and attend her dad's funeral. Even as a few months earlier we had gone to Cleburne for my mother's funeral. I was determined to be there for her.

Sure enough, by the time of the Lakeside AA meeting, I was hitting my stride. No longer depressed, I was into the pink cloud sobriety and it was to last the rest of the decade of the '80s. That otherwise bleak and blah decade was to be the most active and enjoyable in the practice of law for me. The everyday work was more fun and satisfying than any other period.

The strategic alliance with my law partner Brady Coleman was intact and strong. We worked closely together and we bolstered one another through the challenges of that period as never before.

Blanco Street Office

What could I tell Molly about, for example, the 1980s? It was a time of sobriety, serenity and enjoyment of law practice in the house on Blanco Street.

Early in the '80s, Maury Maverick was in the last phase of his law practice before he became a newspaper columnist in San Antonio. His pared-down practice consisted of a few probate cases. I had only vague recollections of the law of estates from law school courses. But he sent us a dilly of a probate case in 1981. It involved a doctor and his wife who were caught in a flash flood on Memorial Day weekend in Austin. There was flooding that killed 13 people, including the doctor and his wife, a nurse. Neither had a will.

Apparently, the government of Hungary contacted a law firm in New York in hopes of getting some taxes from the doctor's estate since his heir was a citizen of that country. The New York lawyers contacted Maury who told them to contact me. We wound up representing the estate of the doctor, but not his wife's.

The only living heir of the doctor was his father who was an old gypsy in or near Budapest. The two had been estranged for years and not even the Hungarian government could find the itinerant gypsy. A creative solution was needed. Sounded to me like a job for a real gumshoe not to mention a gypsy fiddler, Brady Coleman.

So off he went to Hungary on the case and he did–don't ask me how–find the gypsy heir, and I have always pictured them playing fiddles together in the light of the campfire. Music must have transcended the language barrier; the heir signed the papers and his inheritance was set in motion.

With disputes between our client's estate and his wife's estate and the difficulty of selling their condo, the case dragged on for years during which we learned probate law and I continued to handle these cases for the rest of my time as a practicing lawyer. My last appearance in a regular courtroom was in probate court in Austin before my old friend Judge Guy Herman. It is something of a paradox that surprises me in retrospect.

Even in the politically dreadful era that was the 80's, there were some notable cases. We initially worked on a big civil rights case in federal court on behalf of a dynamo of a former school teacher, Evelyn Sell, who was a member of the Socialist Workers Party (SWP). She had been under the surveillance of the ever-vigilant FBI. Agents had secretly gone to her employer, the Austin Independent School District, and gotten her fired from her teaching job. It was part of the disgraceful COINTELPRO dirty tricks operation of the FBI, conceived by "Jedgar" (as we affectionately called him) and operated secretly during the Nixon Administration.

In this nasty business the local Red squad cop, Bert Gerding, had played a role and I got to depose him, finally letting him have it with the questions of decades of his snooping on us. After Evelyn had been subjected to an especially repetitive and relentless deposition–and at that time she was paralyzed and in a wheel chair due to a car accident–I apologized to her on behalf of the entire legal profession, but the FBI lawyers had not upset her. She was tough and intelligent.

Later I joined her case with the larger suit by other plaintiffs and the SWP in Manhattan. I went to New York in the summer of 1981 to play an ancillary role in the large case. The federal judge took something like 7 years to decide it but ruled in favor of the SWP and individuals who had been victimized by the feds.

In 1982, I represented the progressive Citizens Party in a lawsuit that got them on the state ballot that year. It was to be the first of several ballot access cases to come to me in the '80s and into the '90s. I felt an affinity with the Citizens Party, which was made up of progressive people. I have come to believe that we do not have a two-party system. There is one party, the War Party, which is divided into two wings differing only on domestic policy.

I enthusiastically accepted the case on behalf of the Citizens Party because if we are to endure and prevail as a nation, our electoral process must be reformed and include a party that is anti-war and anti-adventurist imperialism, as well as truly progressive on domestic issues. Some other cases on ballot reform I had were really just cases, those things I had to do to pay the overhead.

I never bought into the theory popular with some lawyers that we are just paid gladiators, ready and willing to represent whoever wants us and can pay the fees we ask. I wanted to use my license and skills to represent clients I believed in, respected or even loved in the shared struggle for progressive change, for peace and justice.

In 1988, I represented, along with many other lawyers, the Veteran's Peace Convoy to Nicaragua. Some veterans and religious ministries up north had gotten together truckloads of humanitarian aid and caravanned south heading for Nicaragua. The Sandinista government was not in favor with the Reagan Administration, to put it mildly. Since there was an embargo in place against Nicaragua, the trucks were stopped at the border in Laredo.

Again it was Bill Kunstler who called. The Center for Constitutional Rights was sponsoring litigation on the grounds that humanitarian aid was excepted under the embargo. Kunstler's wife Margie Ratner, a fine lawyer in her own right, was an attorney on the case; the wonderful legal services program, then known as Texas Rural Legal Aid (TRLA), and its director, David Hall, joined in on the legal action against the Government. My status as a private attorney under contract to TRLA was expedited by my good friend of many years, John Muir, who was Director of Private Attorney Involvement for TRLA.

In my view, an almost invincible legal team had been created for this case. Since I knew David Hall and I had been brought in by the Center, I was selected to act as lead counsel in a suit we would file in federal court in Laredo. Shortly, on a hot summer day I went to Laredo to meet with Margie and the team of TRLA lawyers. We worked through the night to put together the pleadings with very substantial help from Michael Ratner and the folks at the Center for Constitutional Rights (CCR) back in New York.

I had worked over the years many times with CCR. They are the greatest legal resource in the country for progressive people and groups. The Center was founded during the civil rights struggle in the '60s. Some very able and smart lawyers have worked there and they have done great things.

The aid convoy case was tried before Judge George Kazen, an excellent federal judge appointed by Jimmy Carter. The narrow legal point which had to do with the exception to the embargo for humanitarian aid and legislative history was well briefed at TRLA and well argued by TRLA lawyer Bill Beardall. In conducting the trial, I put on several witnesses. In the end the court ruled in our favor and the Veterans Peace Convoy was allowed to pass on through the border into Mexico and ultimately to Nicaragua. It was a major "victory for the people".

It was particularly satisfying because a few years before I had gone to Nicaragua as part of a National Lawyers Guild delegation to see first hand the workings of the Sandinista government after the '79 revolution. I was impressed and moved by what I saw. The United States should have been supporting and encouraging the people's government in Nicaragua, far more democratic than most of the regimes we did support around the world, as it struggled to alleviate the acute poverty and widespread illiteracy, which were the legacy of the dictatorship of Samoza.

Instead, we were paying a mercenary group of thugs, who today would be called terrorists, to kill and brutalize Nicaraguans. Known as the contras, they raped, pillaged and murdered with CIA-provided weapons and aid. Because of our legal victory, and more importantly because our clients had collected the cargo of humanitarian aid and bravely set out for Managua, medications and supplies, bicycles to give health and literacy workers some mobility, and many other non-military items got to Nicaragua in that summer of 1988. This was in the sharpest imaginable contrast with the tools of destruction, bloodshed and violence our government was providing to death squads and terrorists in support of all manner of right-wing groups in Central America.

It was legal work that I felt as good about as any I have done in 37 years practicing in Austin. At times like these it was good to be a lawyer; it was indeed the reason I was a lawyer.

Otherwise, my cases in the '80s were civil rights cases for citizens wrongfully imprisoned or brutalized by the police, working people discriminated against in the workplace or fired unjustly, student demonstrators arrested at the university, and always the criminal cases which often involved important constitutional rights–4th, 5th and 6th Amendment issues mostly.

The Ruby Gun Case

Molly is abashed by the sheer size of the mega file of my most publicized case.

It had all started on the 25th anniversary of the Kennedy assassination when I received a call from Earl Ruby, Jack's brother. When Jack died, it was discovered that Jack had more than one will. There was some early litigation about which of the wills was to be probated in the late '60s. The will that was accepted for probate made a Dallas lawyer the executor of Jack Ruby's estate.

The will was written on a Galveston motel's stationery back in the '50s. The lawyer who counseled Jack as he wrote it out by hand was named executor of the estate. He had done nothing at all for 20 years. The estate of Jack Ruby consisted of a handful of items, including a jock strap, that were entombed in a bank safety deposit box. There was no money.

The only item of any value in the estate was the pistol that Jack used to kill Lee Harvey Oswald, and that only because of its historical significance. Earl, on behalf of all Jack's siblings, was trying to remove the lawyer as executor and secure possession of the gun for the family. The ultimate objective was to get the gun.

Earl had been unable even to communicate with the executor/lawyer, now in his `80s, not exactly still sharp. Some said senile. He perversely refused to do anything except serve as "Keeper of the Gun." (He often during the trial voiced proprietary sentiments about the gun, forgetting himself and admonishing a lawyer not to touch the .38, which was an exhibit.)

Of all the lawyers who swarmed about in Jack Ruby's post-conviction court proceedings, Earl most trusted the illustrious Bill Kunstler of New York. Earl called Kunstler first. I had known Bill for 20 years at that time. Kunstler referred Earl to me since it was a Texas case.

I picked up my phone in the Blanco Street office little suspecting what I was about to get into. I was retained by Earl and the 5 or so other brothers and sisters of Jack, to sue for the removal of the old executor. I went to Dallas first to go through the boxes of history that were the old court records. I filed suit shortly afterwards in probate court in Dallas.

Over the following two years there were about five or six pre-trial settings as I honed in on the legal issues in the case and fine-tuned the pleadings by amendments. A couple of experienced probate lawyers and a trial lawyer represented the executor of Jack's estate. Even though it was hard to see anything of value they had done for the estate, they all sought payment of their legal fees from the estate. Under cross-examination the time claimed was shown to be padded, inadequately documented and sometimes inconsistent in the records of attorneys claiming the same work. For example, two of the lawyers would do something together, the time records with which they sought to document the task would vary wildly and they could not explain it.

The spectacle they presented was clear. Here were those damn lawyers with their hands out; the jury was turned off. Also, the jury seemed to feel naturally enough that Jack's property should go to his family, not the swarming lawyers. (We, wisely, I think, sought no fees from the court; we had a contingent fee agreement with the clients.) The legal wrangling culminated on Election Day in November 1990 in a jury verdict in our favor removing the executor, and awarding not a dime in attorney's fees to the old executor or his bevy of greedy lawyers.

The trial lasted a week and a half. My old friend Doug Larson, a Dallas lawyer, assisted at the trial of the case especially in jury selection in Dallas County where he worked. It was an early Court TV case, televised in toto. I cannot remember any trial in my 40 years of being licensed that was more fun. Some were arguably more important, more difficult, more surprising to win. But this case was the most fun.

It took another year of post-trial legal maneuvering to get the historic pistol away from its dotty caretaker. (It had rested in the safety deposit box for all the years after Jack Ruby died.) Earl Ruby auctioned it in New York in December 1991 through one of the big auction houses for $200,000.

By the time the case was tried, Earl had stopped paying my legal fees; my time was certainly accumulating. I agreed to a contingent fee of one-third of the recovery to palliate the wealthy but penurious businessman from Michigan. We had experienced a difference of opinion over whether I should get paid for this mounting time, and we resolved this by agreeing to the contingent fee contract, meaning I took the risk of getting no fee in a case that was a bizarre if historical exercise in American jurisprudence.

As it turned out, Earl would have paid me a whole lot less if he had simply paid an hourly rate. But Earl was afraid to pay the freight for a case that was no sure winner, to say the least. After two years of legal arguments, the case had to be tried to a jury in Dallas where I had grown up and briefly lived again in the early '70s. I was an Austin lawyer but Dallas was familiar turf to an old Adamson High debater.

The verdict we received was 100 percent in our favor; verdicts often are a mixed bag. It was a mighty triumph to send me off with Nancy to Europe (Ireland first and last) for a few weeks of vacation. The idea for taking a longer than usual vacation was generated by the unusual presence of a cash windfall in late 1990. Brady and I sold the magnificent old house on Blanco Street and after 12 years, it produced a good price. In late 1989, Brady had come in one day and told me he was hanging it up, quitting law practice to pursue his acting career, as well as his music–he played guitar and fiddle, probably banjo, and he could yodel. I was dazed by this news. He wanted to cash out on the building. Why didn't I just buy his half interest? I've often wondered since. In fact, it never occurred to me. The era seemed to be over. Selling the building was just part of ending it. Taking the money and blowing it in Europe was the only logical thing to do. Truthfully, I was far from sure I would ever come back to the practice of law. Nancy and I both took the last two months of that year off, in Europe roaming around, and then in Norman, Oklahoma (where my stepson, Nancy's son Tim and his family lived) for the holidays. Thanksgiving in Paris; Christmas in Oklahoma. From the sublime to the ridiculous. But we loved both stays for very different reasons. In Norman while we were abroad our second grandson was born and we could hardly wait to see him.

At the onset of the new decade in 1990, after I tried the Ruby gun case in Dallas and after Brady Coleman, my law partner, quit practice, the profession became more of a burden. No fun, nothing exciting going on with the law.

I had absolutely no idea where my life went from there. But wandering the courthouse environs provided a temporary answer as I happened upon my old friend and former collaborator (in the second suit I brought against the State Bar of Texas), Laird Palmer. He was one of three lawyers who owned a beautiful office, two blocks from the Blanco Street office. Laird offered me an office in the building. The office I took, recently vacated by a disbarred lawyer imprisoned for marihuana possession, was a dream office. The most elaborate, roomy and well-appointed office I've ever had, with a capitol view. In this way, I was nudged along back into the everyday practice of law in a new set-up, quite different from the law commune or my unwritten partnership with Brady.

I was once again actively involved in the love-hate relationship I had with law. I had very few cases to consider when we returned from our long trip. It seemed that the cupboard was bare. Yet, I plunged back in.

For the first time in 20 years, I had no law partners. The office I was in was owned and managed by others. My secretary came with the space in a package deal. Pat Montgomery, a consummate pro, had been our secretary at Simons & Coleman for years and had gone to the District Attorney's Office when she left us, or we left her.

This strangeness was made more bearable by the near-spectacular office

I occupied in the near-spectacular hillside office building in a Spanish motif, and by Laird being around a lot to swap stories with, even though he ostensibly lived on a ranch up in the Hill Country a hundred miles away. All of it was very Austinesque.

In 1991 the Texas legislature effectively wrote lawyers out of the process for workers to obtain compensation for injury and disease on the job and just as they intended, it is now much harder for workers to get fair compensation. They would write us out of all tort litigation if they could.

True, I did become deeply engaged in the tort litigation against repressed memory therapy, or FMS, for about 3 years in the mid-'90s. But I believe we are now in the most stultifying period since the early New Deal Supreme Court days, or possibly ever in our history, for achieving any progress by litigation. Though brave activists still get arrested and need lawyers.

There is an alarming trend to shut off access to the courts by ordinary citizens either through pricing litigation beyond their means, or limiting the liability of insurance companies and big corporate defendants. This is being done under the subterfuge of "tort reform." At the same time, never before in my lifetime have the courts been less sensitive to the constitutional rights supposedly guaranteed to all.

The federal courts went sour long ago. Now we are seeing state courts follow suit. Big insurance and corporate money have succeeded in denying the citizen redress in court by the mythos perpetrated in their PR campaigns: that selfish, unscrupulous personal injury lawyers are filing phony, inflated claims, and that too many people are simply litigious, greedy and malingering, looking for something for nothing. This is nothing more than corporate propaganda.

Yet, the public perception has been irreparably tainted and is being molded to suit big corporate interests. Trial lawyers are seen as vultures, charlatans, ambulance chasers. The lawyer jokes reflect the current image of a once-great profession.

There are many lawyers who are greedy and unprincipled but they are not chasing ambulances–they are to be found in the behemoth firms that represent the big corporations and in corporate board rooms. The noble vision of the lawyer fighting for the rights of average citizens against big business and the state is growing hazy in the polluted atmosphere of the courts as we enter the new millennium. Whence Atticus and Darrow; will they return again?

FMS

Before I trained her as a quadralegal, Molly was more of a mascot. We went to Ireland in 1984 right after we got her. Ellie stayed with her and sometimes she thought Ellie was her owner.

I did screw up and lose my son in 1965. But now I am blessed with boys, grandsons. This is the very best thing about living to be my age. For all the years she was growing up, my daughter was the deepest joy of life for me.

Being close to my daughter, I was rocked by what I saw one of my very best friends go through in the early to mid-90s. I have his permission to go into what happened in depth, from his viewpoint and mine as one who fully supported him during the ordeal. I agreed not to use names. It was clear to me he had been the victim of a false accusation and many others were, also.

A bolt came out of the blue in the summer of 1992 when his adult daughter informed him she was cutting off all contact with him. He was destroyed by this. He came to me for assistance in my dual role as AA sponsor and lawyer. I have rarely seen anyone so devastated–and I see clients who have been seriously injured or who have lost a family member or are looking at years of incarceration.

I did some reading and investigation and learned about the social phenomenon of repressed memory therapy that was started, or catalyzed, by the book "The Courage to Heal" by two "therapists" with low-level credentials but with an agenda. That it happened to thousands of other parents of grown children was little comfort to my client.

A psychologist taken in by this sham had convinced my friend's grown daughter that she "repressed" memory of being sexually abused as a child and he was, through hypnosis, bringing her to "remember" that it was her dad who had molested her. It is likely that some type of molestation occurred when she was very young, a single brief episode perpetrated by a man who came to a party at the home of my client. Significantly, she did remember this incident. But the trendy repressed memory therapy of that period called for a young woman's father to be the main offender.

He was accused but there was no way to confront the accusations, which always remained vague. He could not talk to his daughter or to the "therapists" who refused to see him face to face. To make things worse, he could not see his grandchild.

By Christmas season of 1992, I feared that my friend was suicidal in a sense: in that he was resigned to the fact that he would seek the illusory relief of the bottle. Even though he had accumulated long-term sobriety, he thought, or he would say, knew he was going to drink. The certain knowledge that he would slip and find some fleeting comfort in alcohol took hold of his mind. Even the fleeting comfort would be better than none. (In AA this is called "stinking thinking".)

Each time he was permitted to see his two-year-old grandchild (only in the presence of a designated third party) he came away wondering when and how the drinking would start again. It did not help that it was nearing Christmas, a time alcoholics have difficulty with under normal circumstances.

Then suddenly one night morosely driving home from seeing his grandchild he thought: NO, it's not good enough for me to die like that, for he was certain that if he drank he would die. He believed that absolutely. The grim certainty that he would end up drunk and that it would be the end, left him. He thought it was too pathetic; it reduced his whole life to something unspeakably, pitiably small and devoid of meaning. He had witnessed others in his family die that way, helplessly destroyed by booze. He could not allow it to repeat a generation later.

And so he rebounded from despair, from the certainty of the final big drink. Whether from inner strength or the great principles of AA or the steady support and love of his loyal wife, he got to the other side. The anguish remained until his daughter came back in 1995. The pain was always there for those three terrible years, but he knew after Christmas of `92 that he would go on.

In spring of `93, he and I discovered an organization of the families of victims of the phenomenon that ensnared my close friend's family. False Memory Syndrome (FMS) was what psychiatric and memory experts were calling it. People were banding together and fighting back against the harmful psycho fad, which depended upon hypnosis or other dubious means of "recovering" memories of sexual abuse during childhood.

My friend and his wife (the girl's step-mother) went to Philadelphia to meet with hundreds of such families in a conference and to hear from the best scientific minds in order to learn about and understand this destructive wave in our society. Many, many adult children (mostly daughters) were "recovering" repressed memories of sexual abuse by their parents (mostly dads).

It was toxic therapy bringing destruction of families, greater distress to the young people getting the false memories, leaving them much worse than they had been when they sought therapy. It swept over the country in the late `80s and into the `90s. It was tragic for a large number of families. The three years my friend suffered this scourge took a toll on him that was obvious to me as his sponsor/attorney.

The False Memory Syndrome Foundation, composed of accused families and professionals in mental health and law, was definitely a therapeutic group for him. He organized a local group and they recruited nationally known speakers to come in for meetings. My friend, who is a professional in his regular life, hit the public speaking circuit and would go and speak wherever anyone would listen; he went on the radio and was interviewed by print journalists. He even volunteered a week working on-site in the Philadelphia office of the family group, FMS Foundation.

He almost totally neglected his work for the three years his family was in the grip of this tragedy. The near full-time battle he and his wife waged almost ruined them financially. But that is where my other role came into play. I was a trial lawyer. There were suits being filed; the fight was inevitably moving into the courtroom. I took his case and that turned out to be a significant key to turning the situation around.

The mere fact that he had a lawyer and that we filed suit was enough to scare off the psychologist, who at least stopped being the constant influence trying to engender a memory of something that never happened. These "therapists" were so afraid of the rational examination attendant to a lawsuit that they often folded up the tent and ran.

To my friend what was paramount was getting his daughter back, although he came out well on the financial end as well. It was a fight he never wanted. No family ever would want to have to fight a phony therapy that brainwashed their own child and turned her against them. No one wants to find out what it is like to be falsely accused, by one for whom he has the tenderest love, of committing the foulest crime there is short of murder.

I started taking more cases against the therapists and hospitals who practiced this injurious sorcery. One could say it became my last crusade. A dividend of this I never figured on came to me: there was meaning again in the practice of law. In AA, working to help others has the dividend of helping ourselves and both my client and I were enormously helped by being proactive in the over-all fight against FMS.

But the best was that his daughter was able to escape the serious often life-long suffering caused by this toxic therapy. With the primary source removed, we were able to get his daughter to agree to mediation. We brought in a psychologist named Paul Simpson who had started out to be "one of them"; but seeing the light, he worked to educate people and had had some success mediating between accuser and accused. It was the first breakthrough and made all the rest possible.

My friend was very hesitant about putting his daughter through the wringer of litigation. She was too fragile, and also we did not want to set up an adversarial situation that might solidify her still vague response to the psychologist's suggestions. In the face of having to appear in the neutral setting of the mediation to talk with us, the therapist bowed out, as I said.

Thankfully the daughter began to see a psychologist who turned out to be first-rate. This practitioner did see father and daughter together and the whole business was examined with rationality. She never had any memory of being abused by her dad because it never did or could have happened. With the help of the new therapist worthy of the name, she was able to shed the sick illusion that had been artificially implanted and had enveloped her life and her family's.

By fall 1995 she made a surprise reconciliation visit to the home of my clients; she had not been in the house in which she grew up for over 3 years though it was only a couple of miles from where she lived. In August of 1995, she came over on her own and with that small step, the reconciliation process had begun. This was what my clients had prayed for above all else for three solid years of anguish.

At a time when I was almost totally immersed in the lawsuits against therapists like the one who had led my friend's daughter into the morass of FMS, I was particularly delighted when my own daughter came to work in my law office. Perhaps best of all, she brought my youngest grandson Eric, who was an infant, to my office each day where we had a place all set up for him. It meant that every working day the first thing I saw in the morning was my beautiful infant grandson.

I had gained a new and deeper appreciation of family in my involvement in the fight against FMS. I saw how fragile it all was, how a coincidence of forces–an upset young person getting tied up with the wrong counselor, or a million other things–could shatter a close family. The year Ellie and Eric worked in my office may well have been the best single year of practicing the law I ever had.

My daughter and I had always been close and we now had a new appreciation of that fact as we worked daily to undo the wreckage wrought by so-called therapists hacking through the ties between people with machetes of accusation, estrangement, suspicion and suggestion.

In one of my cases, the young woman had committed suicide. It was the most gut-wrenching case I ever handled in all my decades as a practicing lawyer. Not a day went by that I didn't thank God (my agnostic God) that my daughter was well and with us.

These adult children accusing beloved parents of ignominious betrayal were the primary victims of the iatrogenic disease spawned by therapy; the parents were secondary victims. As will usually happen with such things, the tide turned and the madness of that "therapy" has been recognized and discredited widely in the field of psychiatry (where it had not gotten even the patina of validity), psychology and counseling. It had been most prevalent at the bottom of this totem pole with therapists of dubious credential but supported by a few with professional status.

The battle was almost personal in the beginning as I saw what my close friend and AA protégé had gone through, but it was also social. We fought to keep the tragedy from destroying other families, perhaps permanently, as with my friends and clients who lost their daughter for good when her misery culminated in her hanging herself while supposedly being kept safe in a psychiatric ward. No lawsuit could bring her back to life. Nothing anyone could ever do would stem the suffering Nancy and I saw them go through. And it will only end when they pass from this life.

In our mutual struggle, not just in the courtroom, but in our total lives, I came to love these people as much as I have ever loved clients. Perhaps I came to an even deeper understanding of Kunstler's statement that he loved his clients. In some instances, our lives do become intricately joined in struggle so that we are not objective, detached practitioners, and we hope we never are. For that is what imbues our daily frequently tedious work with its meaning.

It is not unusual to feel this way in the midst of Movement struggles, to stand with our clients and say: they are my sisters and brothers, give them, give us justice. But we had nothing else in common with most of the families I represented in the FMS epidemic, especially the parents of the girl who committed suicide while supposedly receiving help.

The bereaved couple were affluent suburbanites; we live in a modest inner city, racially mixed neighborhood and I did not take a path in law that made us rich, far from it. We were longtime radical activists, veterans of the anti-war and civil rights movements; they were Republicans and he was a Viet Nam vet, who had always believed in the rightness of that defining event of our generation. We were recovering alcoholics; they had rarely had more than one cocktail or glass of wine at a time from what we could tell. They were regular Presbyterian church-goers; we were free thinkers, not religious. We had lived in a sexually free culture and done drugs (those things long in the past tense now). How could our two families have been any more different?

But for the astonishing development in America in the last two decades of the century of repressed memory therapy, or FMS, it is unlikely we would ever have had a thirty second conversation. Yet, in our shared battle, socially as well as forensically, we came to love these people profoundly, and others as well who fell prey to the toxic therapy. In this I think we learned something that many of our political brothers and sisters may never know. In common suffering and struggling to survive a stark tragedy, the non-essentials fall away; and in that dim and grim fight to see tomorrow, a bond at the deepest level of our humanity emerges. AA had showed us something of the same thing, but not quite as poignantly.

As long as I live, I will care deeply about these clients, and all the families we encountered and felt their sorrow in the years the phenomenon went on. For some the sorrow continues.

Lawsuits played a big part in ending the epidemic that caused so many adult children to falsely accuse parents they had once adored of horrible crimes. It was a good fight to fight, a sad fight to have to fight. In the end, I had been glad I was a lawyer, able to call the culprits and dupes to account before a court of law.

The one thing the toxic therapy could not stand was the light of day, close scrutiny, rational examination. On witness stands all across America, the voodoo of recovered memories of childhood sexual abuse crumbled before the eyes of disinterested juries and judges. Some of the worst practitioners made big money from the suffering they inflicted. Now many of them are in prison, have lost licensure, insurability and, the most important penalty of all, lost credibility.

In the three years from 1994 to 1997 I represented many of these families in the most red-white-and-blue remedy the ordinary, singular citizen of the land still has: going to court. It is an endangered remedy as bought-and-paid-for politicians work under the misnomer of "tort reform" to close the door to the courthouse to citizens suing big businesses. Most seem to know not what they are losing in this greedy onslaught led by the insurance industry.

I plied my legal skills on behalf of many of the young people who were swept into the toxic therapy and their families. Lives had been permanently damaged. Caps on damages would have been grossly unjust. Hospitals and clinics were complicit; in some cases they ran the scam themselves for nothing more than the lucre. The therapists and hospitals involved were represented by their insurance companies which had done nothing to prevent the toxic therapy from harming thousands, if not millions, of American families and whose lawyers stopped at nothing in impugning the victims, the patients of their own insureds, in an effort to avoid paying fair damages.

What amount of damages would have compensated our friends who lost their daughter? Going to court for justice, fighting this scourge day in and day out, gave meaning to their shattered lives in those days and in itself saved some lives. The man who had been my dear friend and his good wife fought back and it helped them to survive. I have never in the four decades of fighting in the courts for people's rights been called to apply my efforts and skills to a more noble or exalted purpose. Or one I believed in more passionately.

For a brief moment I saw the benign possibilities of the law, had some of my past faith restored, in the surprising and lamentable development that drove me back to the courts in the mid-'90s. But that fight has been won. The fact that justice prevailed by and large could be seen as an argument for a re-dedication to the law as a vehicle for social change. But I am unconvinced.

It takes much more than progressive and altruistic lawyers to accomplish meaningful and lasting advances. As Arthur Kinoy said, it takes the people in motion. Lawyers alone cannot bring about peace and justice, but the people aroused to action can.

The Last Hurrah

I depend upon Molly to listen to my ideas on handling various legal matters, what few I still have in the waning days of the millennium. There is only Molly to endure my angry outbursts over the daily little fuck-ups that go hand in hand with the managing of the legal disputes we call cases.

In 1999, as I was resigned to contemplating these experiences and letting go of the law, an unexpected thing happened. I was contacted by a group of people in San Marcos, just south of Austin, who had been running a low power FM radio station and been harassed by the long arm of the federal government, the FCC. The group had originally started as a campaign to legalize marihuana, but the low power FM station now served much broader interests.

I had in fact represented one of the leaders, Zeal Stefanoff, in a protest action nearly ten years earlier. He walked into the Sheriff's Office in San Marcos smoking a large joint. That will tend to get you arrested.

At trial we sought acquittal by virtue of jury nullification, i.e. asked the jury to find him not guilty because marihuana should be legal. The Hays County jury did not comply. We were several decades ahead of our time in this.

At that time the group was feeling empowered after winning a federal suit to distribute their newspaper, a slam dunk First Amendment case, ably handled by ACLU lawyer, Patrick Wiseman. Their latest project, the radio station, known as KIND-FM, had taken off, getting wide respect and support from a broad section of the little college town of San Marcos.

The FCC regarded even these low power community stations as under their jurisdiction though how federal jurisdiction applied was a subject of debate and litigation. The controversy was a battle being fought all over the country. Low power FM stations in California, New York, New Jersey, Pennsylvania, Ohio and other states had filed suits against the FCC. The Center for Constitutional Rights (again in the forefront) and the National Lawyers Guild were sponsoring and assisting suits to allow grass-roots groups to operate in a small area as non-commercial community radio without having to get a license from the FCC.

The airwaves are not owned by the government but by the people. Regular commercial stations operated in large interstate areas give rise to federal jurisdiction and justify a federal regulatory scheme. There were two forces at work to defeat the low power stations' bid for the right to be heard. First, the FCC wanted to protect (extend, is what we argued) its turf. They were jealously protecting their asserted jurisdiction over ALL broadcast use of the radio airwaves. Second, there was and is a move by a few powerful corporate groups to gain dominance (or monopoly) in the radio and television industries.

Groups like Clear Channel have moved to gobble up stations and grow into a few big conglomerates seeking ever-greater control of broadcasting. The FCC, under Bush the Younger's Administration, has moved to actually change long standing regulations to make it easier (and legal) for them to do this. One does not have to be a conspiracy buff to become alarmed over this trend.

Coincidentally, these companies are very conservative in their politics. (Just listening to their output confirms that.) They support Bush in his invasions of countries and waging of wars, his plans to destroy the remaining social programs such as Social Security and Medicare by privatizing them, and his abandonment of any governmental protection of the environment while allowing the eco-criminals to drill for oil in parklands. Big corporations seem to believe in big government when they are aided and abetted by the agencies that should be regulating them or they are getting subsidies as the airlines, drug companies, defense contractors, banks and insurance companies have. But they want to be free of government "interference with the free market" when it comes to plundering the environment or gouging the public.

Some voices and views could only be heard on the upstart low power community FM radio stations. All you need to broadcast is a transmitter. The FCC descended like gangbusters on the low power FM stations to protect us all from this dangerous lawlessness. They closed down most of the stations with DEA-style raids, confiscating the equipment, threatening arrest of the people.

In addition to the San Marcos group, there was another station in Canyon Lake, just outside of New Braunfels down the road from San Marcos. Later, a couple more sprang up in Austin. All were smashed by the FCC.

Early in 1999 I sat in my office in Clarksville and listened to the prospective clients from KIND-FM. I wanted to help them and support the laudable work they were doing at the most basic level–in small communities reaching out to a few people. I knew from 35 years of "tilting at such windmills", as a cynical acquaintance put it, that federal lawsuits over important constitutional rights are expensive and time-consuming. These clients were practically penniless, lacking the price of admission to the great American theater of justice: they would be unable even to pay the filing fee.

At this point, I had a notion that was at least worth a shot. I sounded out my old friend John Muir, the capable and savvy director of private attorney contracts for Texas Rural Legal Aid (now, Texas Rio Grande Legal Aid), hoping that there might be a chance that TRLA would sponsor the litigation.

This program was one of the best in the nation and it had stood up to right-wingers in Congress and the board of the Legal Services Foundation (LSF) that funnels federal money to legal services programs. Its director David Hall is a stand-up lawyer of the progressive persuasion with a history of good works.

I had worked under a private attorney contract on the Veterans' Peace Convoy (to Nicaragua) case eleven years earlier. That big victory in court had only brought the vultures in Congress and on the LSF board down on TRLA. But it had survived that and other attempts to throttle or dismantle TRLA. Not just endured, but prevailed.

I feared they would be too gun shy for litigation on behalf of impoverished and embattled low power FM radio broadcasters against the federal government–the hand that feeds TRLA and all legal services programs. I did not see myself involved in one more grand defense of constitutional rights for two rag-tag bands of radio operators. But I was dead wrong about all that.

TRLA did allow me to take the case as a private attorney contractor. That meant they would pay the expenses of the litigation and about 25 percent of my fees which would be all I would get. Nevertheless, this made it possible.

It was fortuitous that the tiny Radio Canyon Lake had come into the client picture and become a plaintiff along with KIND-FM. San Marcos is in the Austin Division of the Western District of Texas, a federal court I knew I did not want to be in because of arch-conservative judges I had locked horns with many times. But Canyon Lake is just barely over into the San Antonio Division of the Western District of Texas. That is where we wanted to be. A chance at least of getting a liberal judge.

I associated the assistance of Bill Fowler, a San Antonio lawyer I had known as a good friend going back to our days at the University. We filed the suit on the day after July 4th (calculated to underline the nature of the case–Free Speech and the Bill of Rights). The case was assigned by random rotation to Judge Fred Biery, the best judge we could draw.

At the time we filed, very few, if any, of the other cases around the country had been decided. The case was litigated for the next five years and in that time, virtually all of the other cases went in favor of the FCC. So there came a time when Judge Biery had to decide our case in the face of many other precedents in other federal circuits that went against us.

The last holdout hope was in the D.C. Circuit, where the Center for Constitutional Rights had been granted an en banc hearing, i.e., before all the judges of the circuit, in the case. Judge Biery held our case in abeyance pending decision in that case and when that went against the community low power FM operators, he waited while a Petition for the Writ of Certiorari was presented in the U.S. Supreme Court. It was denied. The judge really had no choice but to rule with the FCC since every case had gone that way.

All was not lost, however. After the years of litigation, the U.S. Congress authorized and the FCC adopted a procedure for approving (not really distinguishable from licensing) small low power FM radio stations, and many have now been "granted" the right to go on the air. A right that has always been there (but without a remedy to effectuate it), in my view not subject to the largesse of the central government.

Our clients were deemed outlaws not entitled to a license under the new rules because they had broadcast in defiance of the FCC, in the case of KIND-FM, for a long time. The federal courts had allowed the FCC to protect its turf, even to that extent. We had fought them for 5 years. At some future time when conditions are different, my clients, among the pioneers in this struggle, may be further vindicated.

The people who exercise their rights, push the limits wrongly imposed and broaden the actualization of the words so solemnly recorded in the Bill of Rights do the greatest service for the freedoms of all of us. These clients are in that category and I salute them.

As the 21st century brought a drastic shift to the right of the central government and we move further than ever down the road of imperialism or dominionism in foreign affairs, the federal courts are backing further away from their traditional role of interpreting the Constitution–the most important function of the third branch of government.

Conservatives decry so-called activist judges making policy or "legislating". But without judges willing to interpret the Constitutional guarantees in light of real world fact situations, we would still have segregated schools. They conveniently look the other way if such "judicial activism" serves their purposes, e.g. the outlandish Supreme Court decision in Bush v. Gore that appointed Bush president even though he lost the election.

The legal profession lost one of its greatest when Warren Burnett died in 2002 after having given his summation of what he thought of law practice and why he was retiring back in 1993 at the State Bar convention. On that occasion it was my honor to introduce him with a perverse combination of hero worship, tomfoolery and ribbing about his having gone to Baylor Law School. (UT Law grads and others in the legal profession think of Texas as the gold standard in our state.)

The speech he gave, as always entirely extemporaneously, should have been published for all lawyers and law students to read. Listening to it should have entitled us to credit toward the mandatory Continuing Legal Education hours required of every lawyer under 70. It seemed to him and to me that many of our colleagues have forgotten the lesson of Atticus Finch and left their honesty and basic decency behind in their pursuit of money.

Congress has defaulted to the executive branch even to the extent of ceding its power to declare wars. The central government is spending taxpayers' money to propagandize, federal agencies are following the party line and discarding solid science, the threat of terrorism is being exploited to justify curtailing of our fundamental rights, the central government is sending representatives to the United Nations who want only to subvert it; even our elections have taken on the taint of doubtful fairness and proper vote counting. After two centuries, this republic is in crisis. I have difficulty imagining what the practice of law will be like if the courts keep getting more and more reactionary.

*

Molly accompanied me now through the long days of the week. She knew what time it was. At 5 p.m., she would leave the "office," a room where I have computer equipment, phones and desk in my house in the 'ville. Molly would begin her campaign imploring me to take her for a walk outside down to the tiny park. She always knew when it was time to go.

On a gray and rainy Tuesday in November, as quietly and gently as she did everything, Molly closed her eyes, lowered her head and died after eighteen and a half years of gracing our home. Without my trusted quadralegal, I have chosen not to go on practicing the law; it would not be the same. But I felt that the course of the years, my experience of the law in the last decades of a century and a millennium, during the most exciting time to be a people's lawyer in the history of America, was worth writing. And so I have.

Epilogue: Bold Marauders

Bold Marauders, the softball team, became Bold Marauders, the benevolent wacky urban gang. We were a fun-loving bunch that included several lawyers, a doctor or two, professors, grad students, ne'er-do-wells, political organizers, all manner of Austin characters. The annual game became the stuff of Austin lore of those grand years of the '60s and '70s. Sometime in the later years of the game, a huge group picture was taken. A print of it was given to me on my 50th birthday a decade after the last game.

Every year on Memorial Day weekend, I still have the urge to get out and get limbered up preparatory to playing second base at the Bold Marauders game. While for over 20 years since the last game ended there have been rumors rampant both in area pubs and AA meetings that a reunion game would occur, it never has. Both teams have had deaths in their ranks. If a reunion game is ever played, it will have to be dedicated to the fallen among us. The original players for both teams are scattered now, too.

Time changes all. But make no mistake, there are still more than a few of us around.

http://boldmarauder.com

About the Author

Jim Simons graduated from the University of Texas Law School in 1965. He worked for the Office of Economic Opportunity (OEO), the federal War on Poverty agency, in its heyday. He then opened a private practice in Austin representing many activists of the New Left. He was a trial lawyer in Texas for nearly four decades, handling many cases involving civil rights and civil liberties. He still lives in the Clarksville neighborhood in Austin with his wife Nancy and their current dogs, Harlow and Max.

www.ingramcontent.com/pod-product-compliance
Lightning Source LLC
Chambersburg PA
CBHW071501080526
44587CB00014B/2176